Little Boy Lost.

*I Don't Know Where I'm Going,
But I'm On My Way.*

Clive Webb

Copyright © 2016 Clive Webb
All rights reserved.

My Memoir

My true life story, from when I was a little boy, escaping death when my dad took his own life in the most horrific way. They say he was suffering from depression, but when I look back and try to piece the jigsaw together, there was more to it than just depression. I was diagnosed with bipolar disorder in 2015, but didn't know I've had this all my life. I needed to get my story out there while I'm in the frame of mind to do so. This book will take you on a roller coaster ride, which is called *My Life*.

Table of Contents

Introduction	7
Little boy lost	9
Strange going on	19
Things must be getting bad	26
The fire	34
The aftermath	44
School years	52
Moving again	69
Marathon man	82
Holiday mode	117
Recession	145
Becoming a dad	167
RIP Mum	180
A chip off the old block	186
Train crash	193
Mirror mirror on the wall	240
Summary	249

Introduction

I am writing this book in an attempt to piece a jigsaw puzzle together which is called *My Life*. Since I was diagnosed with bipolar disorder, I've been trying to understand what my dad was going through. The reason I mention "Jigsaw puzzle" is, in 1972, a couple of months before I was seven years old, my father took his own life after two previous attempts. This was never really spoken of, but all I know is he was suffering from depression. But as parts of the puzzle are falling in place, I'm starting to see the picture. My older sister had certain issues as a teenager but never wanted to speak about it. Certain issues my mother had told me about regarding my dad, all point towards something more than depression alone. Maybe if I could (but this will never be) understand better what my dad was going through, I might be able to understand myself better. It's ironic really that I've always disliked writing, and here I am writing. Well that's it for the intro; I hope you enjoy my first book.

Little boy lost

The reason I have called this book *little boy lost* is because when I was a young boy that's what my mum called me. I was constantly bored and would say, "Mum, what can I do, I'm bored". My mum would reply, "Clive, you are like a little boy lost, I think you miss your brother". I had an identical twin brother who died at birth. There were complications whereas we were both trying to be born at the same time.

My brother's umbilical cord got wrapped around his neck, and sadly he was strangled. If the complications had happened nowadays they probably would have been able to do an emergency caesarean. But back in 1965, they didn't have the kind of sophisticated technology they do now. "I don't know where I'm going, but I'm on my way" is my life. I can remember as far back to when I must have been three or four years old. We lived in a three bedroom semi-detached bungalow. I would play out the front on my tricycle and ride up and down the road. Back then it was safe for young children to play outside unsupervised, there weren't many dangers as there are today. I must say that a lot of what happened back then are quite vague, I don't know if it's because I can't remember, or I have blocked a lot out of my mind. I'm writing down what I can remember when I was at a very young age.

My sister is nine years older than me, although we have a good relationship now, that wasn't the case back then. She was a very spiteful young girl, one instance I can remember was she writing out a birthday card for mum. She asked me to write a kiss on the card, but because I did it wonkily, she kicked me between the legs, bearing in mind that I was only around four to five years old at the time. She would play a school game with her dolls, where she would play the teacher and her dolls were her pupils. She would then take all of the dolls clothes off, line them all up face down, then she would beat them with a copper rod.

When my mum asked why she was doing this, my sister replied that the dolls weren't paying attention to her and were misbehaving, so they needed to be punished.

One other thing that I remember was what my sister did one cold winter night, she walked down to the bottom of the garden and started talking to the trees. She was in her nightdress, it was freezing cold, and she would repeat, "Is anyone there, is anyone there?" Years later when she was asked about all of this, she said, she was attention seeking. She was a nightmare in school; the head teacher lived a couple of streets away from us. One day my sister got into trouble at school, so she went around to where the teacher lived and offered to wash her car. The teacher must have thought that this was out of character for my sister, but let her wash it anyway. But instead of washing it she took out a key and run it up and down the wing of the car, and did quite a lot of damage to the paintwork.

Another instance when she was a teenager, she coaxed another girl into a field where she had a stick. She then made the girl take her clothes off and lay in some stinging nettles, my sister then told the girl if she tried to get out, she would hit her with the stick. Her school advised my parents that she needed professional help and she did spend a week in a mental health unit. But to this day she is still in denial and puts it down to attention seeking. I remember my mum saying that when I was a new born baby, and I was in the cot next to her. In the middle of the night my sister came into the room and stood over me in the cot. My mum said my sister didn't say a word, she just stood there looking at me. My mum then asked her what was she doing, but it was like she was sleepwalking and didn't say a word. My mum then told her to go back to bed, she then just turned around and walked out of the room.

This is something I can't remember, but it's what my mum told me. One day my mum, sister and I, walked down to a pond that was at the bottom of our road. When we were there my sister couldn't get her own way at something, then she started to get spiteful towards mum. Bearing in mind that my mum was the easiest going person you could meet, too easy going in my eyes. We ended up going back home, which was about a mile walk. All the way home my sister was whipping the back of my mum's legs with a stick that she found.

My mum kept telling her off but the more she scolded her, the more my sister did it. When my sister got a bit older and had arguments with my mum, it used to come to blows. Well that's a bit about my sister, I've probably missed a few other instances, but like I said earlier, I've either blocked it out or can't remember.

Well, now a bit about my dad. I can't remember too much about him, he pretty much did his own thing. My parents had separate bedrooms for as long as I can remember, my mum had her TV in her bedroom and my dad pretty much lived in the lounge. I'm going to start with what my mum told me about him before I was born. He left home at a young age as did his two sisters. I think it was because he couldn't stand seeing his dad being henpecked by his mum. My mum told me that my dad said, THERE'S NO WAY I WOULD EVER LET A WOMAN TREAT ME LIKE THAT. When my parents first married they lived in London. My dad did various jobs as he couldn't stick at one thing for too long.

One particular day he had an idea, he would start his own business making babies shoes. So he bought all the necessary equipment that he needed, he didn't go for anything cheap either, it had to be the top of the range equipment, he then set it all up in his garage. My mum told me that they were doing quite well, the orders were coming in, so much so that they had to employ two people. What's better than that, he had his own little business that was doing quite well, he was his own boss with no one to answer too.

But this didn't last long, one particular day my dad just broke down in tears. He said that he could not handle the pressure anymore, he wanted to pack it all in. So that's what he did, he sold off all the equipment and went back working a nine to five.

Now at this point I'd like to say, this to me looks like he may have had a manic episode, now he is coming down from that spell of mania. Who knows what else may have been a manic episode prior to my mum knowing him. That's all I really know about him before I was born. What I do remember about him is that he would spend days if not weeks making things.

One time in particular was when we needed a new fence, then my dad decided to do this himself. He bought all the panels and posts that he needed and built the fence by himself. I don't know how long he was out there, but it was a good few days. When he finally finished it my mum said it looked brilliant, but not in my dad's eyes, he said there was one wonky panel that he spotted.

So instead of taking one panel out to straighten it, he pulled the whole lot down, and started all over again. He started to take his projects into the house, he would have engine parts all over the lounge floor, where he would be dismantling them, then putting them back together. I think this is one reason my mum had enough, she found it hard to live amongst all the mess.

My mum said that he was a perfectionist, everything had to be spot on. Even down to his moustache, if he could not get it to look just the way he wanted it too, he wouldn't go out. One other thing, he was very self-conscious of was his foot. When he was a young boy, he stood on some broken glass which cut an artery in the arch of his foot. After that he never could put his heel fully down on the floor. So he had to have a built up heel in one of his boots.

Strange going on

Don't get me wrong here, I'm not saying the house was haunted, but what I'm about to say, I can't explain. All I can say is there was something very strange going on in that bungalow. But before I go any further, I must stipulate that what I'm about to write did happen. This is what my mum said to me when I was older. One night she got into bed, where I was in the cot next to her. If I can remember rightly she said it was fairly late. She was laying there for a while, tossing, and turning, finding it difficult to go to sleep.

She was lying on her side then decided to lie on her back. At this point, she saw (or what she thought she saw) a white figure standing at the foot of her bed. My mum described this figure to be quite plump with a fairly long nose. The first thing my mum did was pulling the covers up over her head and froze there for a minute.

She said that she started to sweat quite a bit even though this was in the winter and very cold. She then plucked up the courage to peer over the covers to take a second look, but the figure had vanished. She then jumped out of bed to go and tell my dad, who was sleeping in the lounge. My mum always swears blind that she was not dreaming as she hadn't even managed to go to sleep when she saw it. She said that the figure slightly resembled her grandmother who had passed away a long time ago.

I remember my mum talking about this when I was a lot older, she said the very next night she was laying there, obviously, she couldn't sleep after what she saw the night before. Then she heard the door handle creak, so she looked over at the door, which started to open very slowly. She then said all she saw was my dad's head appear from behind the door, in the hope of seeing this figure for himself, she used to laugh about that. I had a strange unexplainable encounter too.

I must have been around 5 years old and I was watching TV with my mum in her bedroom. I needed to go to the toilet so I got up and left the bedroom. In our bungalow, there was a long hallway from my mum's room to the lounge and kitchen. The toilet was on the right about half way down, the lounge was on the left at the other end.

Now I know that this sounds hard to believe, I'm still trying to work this out in my head now, at 50. My dad was in the lounge at the time, then I saw this eye (yes an eye) looking back down the hallway. It was an eyeball on the lounge doorframe, my first thought was it's my dad playing a trick on me, I thought he had it on the end of a stick or something.

So I said out loud, dad stop mocking around, laughed, and went to the toilet. When I came back out, the eye was still there, but then I noticed the lounge door was closed. Being only five, I didn't think much of it and went back to watch TV with my mum. The figure at the foot of the bed and that eye were never seen again.

What with my sister being so spiteful, I must have thought this was the way to behave. The reason I say this is because one day I went to buy some sweets from the corner shop, which was literally two doors away. As I walked towards the door there was a pram left outside the shop, I could hear the baby gurgling in the pram, then the most horrible thought came to me that I'm so ashamed of now. I thought "What if I go over and slap the baby", just because he/she was making silly noises. I never did it, but I thought it, and I don't know why that terrible thought ever entered my head.

I can remember my first day at school, God, I hated it, I was there for a couple of hours and I had enough. There was a tin of money on my teacher's desk, this was the dinner money collection tin. When the teacher left the desk unattended, I went over and took some money out, I only took about 10/20 pence. Then calmly walked out of the school and up to the shops to buy some sweets, which was about 800 meters away.

I was quite happy sitting on a bench outside the shop eating my sweets, when another teacher from the school spotted me. I was then marched back to school where I had a right telling off for walking out of school. I just did not want to be there, I didn't know any of the other kids, it was full of adults that I didn't know, and I wanted to go home. I couldn't wait to get out of the place that day.

I can remember that my dad only drank alcohol once a year at Christmas, and he used to get a little bit drunk. I can remember being in the lounge with him and he put me on his shoulders, then he started dancing around the room to some music that was playing from the TV. My head kept hitting the ceiling because he was jumping up and down, but I didn't mind this as it was fun, I can't remember him ever playing with me like this before.

After that, he probably went back to hiding himself away making something. I think he made all our furniture himself, I know he made our three piece suite and a bed, he was very handy like that.

He would also only work for six to eight months a year, save enough money to take the rest of the year off. Then go and find a new job when his money was getting low. Back then you could find work anywhere.

Like I said before he couldn't stay in the same job for too long before getting bored with it, then he would have to move on to do something else, to me this sounds like bipolar disorder.

Things must be getting bad

I must have been five or six years old when I saw my dad being wheeled out in a wheelchair by paramedics, watching the ambulance drive off with him. I don't know if this was his first attempt at taking his own life or the second. All I know is that at one attempt he took an overdose, and on the other, he tried to electrocute himself in the bath, but I don't know what order he did it in.

I'm not even sure how long he was in the hospital, nothing was really spoken about back then, or if I was too young to fully understand what was going on. It must have been several months later when things just got too bad and my mum decided to leave my dad and take me with her. I don't know why, but my sister stayed with my dad, and my mum and I went into private lodgings.

Well, all I can say is I think I would have been treated better if I was in a concentration camp. We shared a house with a family of three; the couple had a boy who was the same age as me. The woman in that hell hole ruled with an iron fist. At the time, my mum went along with their rules for a while, I never blamed her as she must have been in turmoil at the time, and did not know which way to turn, this was her only option.

I usually had to be in bed at 7pm on the dot along with her son. We shared a room with two single beds. As soon as we were in bed there was to be no talking, no whispering, anything.

The boy, Robert was his name, used to talk and whisper to himself, then his mum would come barging in to shout at us, he would then say it was me and I used to get the blame. I used to have a problem with wetting the bed, which his mum knew about before we moved in. So she would put a rubber sheet under the cotton sheet on the bed.

The first night I wet the bed I got up to go to the bathroom. She must have heard someone up, so she came out of her room to see what was going on. When I told her what happened, she marched me back into the bedroom pulled the cotton sheet off the bed and said "You better not wet the bed again", then she slapped the back of my legs and made me lay on the cold wet rubber sheet for the rest of the night, fucking bitch.

Sorry about that but I'm actually getting angry thinking about that woman as I'm writing this. I had to change schools and go to the same one as Robert. I didn't want to do this as I hated school as it was, let alone changing them. I remember my first day, we were all walking there as it was quite close to where we lived. There was my mum and I, then him and her, I say that because I don't even like writing their names down. As we approached the school entrance I hesitated, I was not going to go in.

My mum tried to speak to me nicely and took my hand, but I still was having none of it. Then the woman took hold of my other hand, and said to my mum, I think we need to be cruel to be kind. Then started to make me walk holding on to my hands tightly, my mum was trying to pacify me, while the other woman was talking to me nicely, which was for my mum's benefit, but she was squeezing my hand really tight so it hurt, and she knew it.

I can't remember how long I was at that school, or stayed in that hell hole of a house. One day I visited my dad, I can't remember if I went home, or we met up. But what I remember is him saying if I come back to live with him, I won't have to go back to school. I thought this was great, no more school which I hated so much, plus I hated it in that house. So when I went back to my mum, I said to her that I want to go back home.

So that's what happened, my mum found new lodgings as she hated it there as well, and I went back home to live with my dad and sister. When I got home I thought this was great, I don't have to go to school anymore. When I reminded my dad about this, he said that I will still have to go until I was 16. I thought, why did you say that I didn't have to go, but now you're saying I have to, I could not understand why he would lie to me. Thinking back now, he was probably trying to get my mum to come back home, it was his only way to win her back, I'm sure he did love her, but he had some serious issues and needed to seek professional help. I don't know if he was ever diagnosed with anything other than depression, was he? Did he know he had problems, or was he in denial?

I was seemingly back there for around 5 to 6 months, the only reason I know this is that it says so in the newspaper, which I will be explaining in the next chapter. Those five to six months I was back there are just blank in my mind. I cannot recall anything in that period, apart from my dad cooking me eggs and chips for dinner and playing this song over and over, he said that it was his favourite song.

Whenever I hear it now, it chokes me up, as the words to the song were what my dad was thinking at that time. It's called, 'Without You', by Harry Nilsson, please listen to it on YouTube, as it makes you better understand how my dad felt at that time. My sister had a boyfriend so I didn't see a lot of her, I can't even remember visiting my mum, but I must have. Can't I remember? Or have I erased it from my memory?

Happier times, my mum &dad's wedding photos, must have been around 1950.

The fire

Now, this is vivid in my mind from when I came out of school. My dad must have dropped me off at school, but couldn't remember that, but I was there as my dad picked me up when school finished. We got in the car, then he said to me, "How do you fancy having a big bonfire", I said yes please, I thought this is not the 5th of November but what the heck, it will be fun.

My dad said the reason we are having the bonfire is that he had a lot of old rubbish that needs burning. He then said he needs to stop at the service station to buy some petrol to get the fire started, so off we went. We stopped at the service station and he got out and went to the boot. He then filled about four or five gallon cans and strapped them in the boot.

We had about a three-mile journey to our house, I can't remember if he spoke or not in the time it took to arrive. We got out of the car then my dad went to the boot to unload the cans. I thought he was going to take the cans around the side and into the back garden. But he didn't, instead he took them straight into the house, so I followed him inside.

Then he undid the can lids and started to throw the petrol everywhere, the floor, the walls, and all over the furniture. Then he turned and looked at me and said, "Right son, let's have a big bonfire". He produced his lighter and asked me if I wanted to light the fire.

I was about to say yes when I heard someone come in the front door, it was my sister and her boyfriend. I could see by their faces and the tone of their voices that something wasn't right. They pleaded with him, and tried to talk him out of what he wanted to do. But it was no good, he had made up his mind, my sister and her boyfriend then grabbed hold of me, and said "We need to GET OUT NOW!" By this time even though I was only 6 years old, I knew what my dad wanted to do. I said to him not to do it, then he said to me not to worry, he will be coming out in a minute. Then my sister grabbed my hand and we rushed out, then went across the road to her friend whose parents owned a hardware store.

All I heard after that was a whooshing sound, a crackling sound, then a loud explosion, all this time I was standing there watching this happen. Then with the explosion the windows shattered. All my neighbours came running out of their houses shouting and screaming. Now I saw smoke pouring out of the shattered windows, and seeping through the roof tiles. It wasn't long before the flames were billowing out of the windows, and at one point they must have been 15ft above the roof line. There were people standing opposite me crying,

I later found out they were crying for us, as they thought we were still in there. While I was standing there witnessing all of this, I was thinking "Where is my dad, he said he will be out in a minute". I don't know how long it took before the fire engines turned up, but it seemed like ages. The reporters showed up and wanted to speak to me and my sister. They wrote in the paper, "Daddy says he is going to set light to himself", which was not true, why would we say that if we were standing there waiting for him to come out, I think they just added that as it sounds more dramatic. That was the last time I saw my dad.

What I can't get around my head is, did my dad want to take his own life along with mine? Once he lit that lighter the whole house must have been engulfed in flames within seconds. I was seconds away from lighting that fire until my sister came in with her boyfriend and managed to get me out. It wasn't until I was older that I learnt that my dad was in court fighting for custody of me on that day.

My mum told me that he turned up with no legal help as he wanted to represent himself. She told me that she actually felt sorry for him, as he was ripped to shreds by her representatives. She said they were bombarding him so much, that he got so tongue tied and could not speak. It made the front page of the papers which I have kept photocopies. These copies are quite blurred so it is very hard to read the small print. Plus you can just make out that the paper states I was seven years old, but I was actually six at the time.

EVENING OF HORROR

KEVIN John, 17, went to see his girl friend Julie. He was just in time to lead her and her young brother from their Bowers Gifford home before it burst into flames.

Julie's father, Charles Webb, had used petrol to set light to the house.

A coroner at Brentwood on Friday recorded a verdict of suicide on Mr. Webb, 51. He died in his blazing home after an explosion shot flames through the roof.

Kevin John, a labourer of Collingwood Road, Basildon, said he called at the home to wait for Julie, Mr. Webb's 16-year-old daughter.

Upset

"Mr. Webb was very upset — he said he felt like burning the house down. That day he had been to court and had been separated from his wife, and he said she had got custody of the children."

"Julie came back from work and said her father was splashing petrol about the house. He said it was his 'last fling against society.'

Explosion

"I tried to reason with him, and I thought of trying to drag him out of the house. But I just got Julie and Clive, his six-year-old son, out and took them over to a shop opposite."

"As I went back there was an explosion. The house was burning. Someone tried to get in the front and someone went to the back, but could not open it because the flames were burning so much."

"I could smell petrol — he had been splashing it everywhere out of petrol cans."

Mrs. Eunice Webb, the dead man's wife, said: "We had been to court that day and were separated. I saw him at the court, but did not speak to him. He seemed all right,

but he left in
"He had
life before,
overdosed of
had to be tak

Dr. John
sultant at St
tal, Billerica
from shock

Dr. Cha
roner, said
domestic
day, and
sprinkled
house, se
perished i
satisfied
life."

A father's 'last fling' ended in death blaze

A GIRL watched in horror as her father splashed petrol about their home. He told her: "This is my last fling against society."

Minutes later, after she and her brother had fled into the street, 51-year-old Mr. Charles Webb put a match to the petrol. An explosion ripped through the bungalow in Pound Lane, Bowers Gifford, and flames shot 15 feet into the air.

Dr. Charles Clark, the Essex coroner, said at the inquest on Mr. Webb: "There had been domestic unhappiness that day, and he was upset.

"He sprinkled petrol round the house, set fire to it and perished in the flames. I am satisfied that he took his own life."

Labourer Kevin John, 17, of Collingwood Road, Basildon, said he called at the house for his girl-friend Julie, Mr. Webb's 16-year-old daughter.

He said: "Mr Webb was very upset — he said he felt like burning the house down.

New-image hospital throws the doors open

THE message to the 600,000 people in Warley Hospital's catchment area is a simple

I found out when I was a bit older that they found my dad's body (what was left of him) in the hallway. For what I could make out, he was lying between the hallway and the lounge. This was where he asked me to light the fire, and that's the spot where he stood when we left the house. This was right below where I saw (or thought I saw) that eye.

Plus I should have added this earlier in the book, but events are coming back to me as I'm writing this. After my mum saw that figure standing at the foot of her bed, she went to see a clairvoyant. She was in a hall full of people and they picked her out. They told her that she had a guiding spirit and that this spirit was watching over her.

Don't get me wrong I'm not saying that I believe in all this, but there is another instance that I will explain later on in this book. It just all seems very strange to me and it's something I cannot explain.

The aftermath

After that horrific day, we were officially homeless. My mum and I stayed with my nan, while my sister stayed with her friend. This is another part of my life that I cannot remember a lot about. The one thing that does stick to my mind is this thin old man coming into my nan's flat. At first, I did not know who this person was as I've never seen him before, he introduced himself as my granddad, this was my dad's dad. I can't remember what he spoke about, but just before he left he gave me a brand new £1 note.

This was a lot of money for a six year old boy in 1972. I don't even know if my other nan was alive or had passed on at that time. When my granddad left, that was the last time I ever saw him. I don't know how long we stayed with my nan, but we were housed in two bedroom maisonette. So my sister and I had to share a bedroom, which I don't think she was too happy about being a 16 year old girl. She was still having anger issues and having arguments with my mum, so much so that they were coming to blows in some instances.

I reluctantly returned to school to receive an over friendly welcome from the teachers and pupils alike. I can remember on that first day, sitting at my desk with this other boy who was my friend (he was actually my ex-next-door neighbour who must have witnessed the fire on that day), he stood up and walked to the front of the class, he stood next to the teacher, and then they presented me with a large box of toys.

The school did a collection for me as everything I owned was lost in the fire, all my sister and I had was the clothes on our back. I know I should have been grateful but I was so embarrassed, all I wanted to do was run out of the class, but I reluctantly accepted the toys and said, "Thank you". Now, what I'm about to say is vivid in my mind, and it couldn't have been so long after the fire.

Where I now lived was not very far away from the bungalow, I would say it was around two miles as the crow flies. In-between the two properties were fields, so I found myself walking towards my old house, across a couple of fields, down a narrow lane, then I found myself about 400 meters down the road from my old house. I don't know why I wanted to go back there, but I just did.

I recognised the house on the corner of the lane I'd just walked down, so I needed to turn right and walk up the road. I walked about 200 metres then I could see the place up on the other side of the road. I finally approached my old home, which I can only describe as a burnt out shell. It looked very eerie as I stood in front of the metal fencing that was erected in front of the house. This must have been on a Sunday as there were no workers or anyone about. Then I found myself squeezing through a gap in the fence, I just made it through.

There were lots of burnt bits of timber and debris on the front lawn, which I had to clamber over. I made it to the front door which was missing, there was a polythene sheet over the doorway which I managed to squeeze through. I stood there in the hallway and looked around, everything was black with soot.

I thought it looked a lot lighter in there than it did before, even though everything was black. I looked up and realised why the ceiling was missing, I could see the sky through the burnt and chard rafters. Then I started to walk down the hallway towards the kitchen and lounge, I looked into my bedroom which was on the right. Everything was gone apart from a heap of burnt wood lying on the floor which were the remains of my chest of drawers.

Then I turned around and saw the lounge, the door was missing there too. Then at that point I realised where I was standing. I was standing on the exact spot where my dad asked me to light the fire. Although I was nearly 7 years old and I thought I was a big boy now, it hit me. Am I standing on the exact spot where my dad perished? I just stood there and tears began to roll down my cheeks, I think at that point the dawn of realisation started to kick in. I wanted to leave. Just before I approached the front doorway, my sister's room was on the right.

I thought I will just quickly look in there before I leave. When I peered into the room, it looked pretty much like mine, then I spotted something on the window sill, it was my sister's favourite ornament, a little brown dog. Half of it was a bit chard and black, but I put it in my pocket to take home. This was the only item of memory we had left from the house.

I walked outside, climbed through the gap in the fence, I still had tears rolling down my cheeks, and ran all the way home, holding on to the little dog in my pocket. I wanted a big cuddle from my mum, and for her to tell me everything will be ok.

When I arrived home, I ran to my mum and flung my arms around her. She got very worried as I didn't really do cuddles, she then asked me what was wrong.

When I told her where I had been, she was quite angry at first, as she thought I was playing around a friend's house further up the street. I forgot all about the little dog I had in my pocket, and went upstairs. I saw my sister in the bedroom getting ready to go out, then that jogged my memory about the dog. Before I took the dog out of my pocket, I told my sister where I had been, she didn't believe me and told me to stop lying.

Then I took her little dog out of my pocket and said, "Look what I've got, your favourite little ornament". She looked at the charred little dog then let out a gasp and said, "Oh my god you are not lying", then she started crying and put her arms around me

School years

A year or two had passed and my mum met someone else. He seemed okay at the time, and before long they got married. He was a practising Catholic and we were not religious in the slightest. Like I said he seemed okay for a while, but I don't think he understood what we had been through. My mum was so easy going, I think she thought that she needed to make things up to us for not being there at that difficult time.

He had a bad time with his father when he was a boy and wondered why my mum used to let us get away with things. Anyway, I won't bore you with the little details, the bottom line was, we didn't get on. My sister hated him, and she wasn't afraid of letting him know. I can particularly remember one night my sister and I were watching 'Steptoe and

Son' on TV, I used to love that program. He came in and said it was getting late and I should be going to bed. I was sitting next to my sister at the time and she said, "No, he's not going to bed, we are watching TV".

Well that made him quite angry and raised his voice. So I wanted to get up and go to bed, then my sister put her arm around me and said to me, "No, you stay there and watch the TV". Then that made him even angrier, so he came over and tried to pull me up. So, there I was like a 'stretch armstrong', one person pulling one arm and another pulling the other. It was like this most of the time.

I think my mum started to regret ever marrying him. One day, she told me one of the reasons she got married, was that she wanted a father figure for me. Don't get me wrong, he was alright some of the time, I think there was a bit of jealousy there. He used to see my mum spoiling me, which was one thing he didn't have when he was a boy. By this time, I had changed schools to one that was close to where I lived. I made a couple of new friends that lived nearby, which was good for me as I didn't mix that well, especially in group situations. I still detested school and would do anything to get out of going.

We moved again into a three bedroom house, I thought this was great as I would have my own bedroom. This place was literally about 200 metres away, so still only a three-minute walk from my school. A few years had passed and I was fast approaching my 11th birthday and it was time for me to go to a comprehensive school. At the time, we could pick who we wanted to sit next to, and I had two friends from the juniors that I picked. It was time for my first day in big school, I had my uniform on and ready to go. The first day was great, we had such a laugh with me clowning around making my friends giggle.

The more I made people laugh the more I used to clown around, but it didn't last long. The teachers wanted to split us up as we were doing more clowning around than working. So they decided to move me to another class where I didn't know anyone, this turned out to be a major problem for me. And at this point I would like to say, all my life I've blocked these events from my mind. As I'm writing this it's like a light bulb just lit up in my mind.

I don't think the teachers knew my background, and I'm certain they wouldn't have known what happened with my dad. But from a very young age I've been moved from pillar to post, I have had to live with this family in what I described as a hell hole. I've had to change schools which was a big deal for me, I've witnessed my house explode into flames with my dad burning to death. I've just got settled and I'm fairly happy, and these teachers want to knock me down just as I'm getting up off the floor and dusting myself down.

Well FUCK THEM, I'm not going back to school, so I tried my hardest to get out of going. My mum was very easy going with me, and I would pull the wool over her eyes and used to say I didn't feel well. This went on for ages and I tried every trick in the book. Even down to mashing up some breakfast cereal with water, then tipping it on my bedroom floor and saying that I've been sick. If I was made to go to school, I would play truant and sit in a field somewhere. My mum would have the school authorities knocking on the door, asking as to why I'm absent. It seemed like I had a phobia for school, I hated everything that it stood for. I hated lessons, physical education, the teachers, pupils (apart from my friends), you name it, and I hated it.

One day I went to the extreme measures of taking some pills, and cutting my wrists. The pills were only some iron tablets, and when I say my wrists it was only on top of them. I think I was too scared to actually go through with taking my own life, but I was trying to prove a point. I wanted to let people know that this is how much I hated school. I wanted to let them see that I was willing to try to commit suicide, rather than going to that place.

When my mum realised what I had done, she immediately rushed me to the doctor. After an examination and a lot of questions, the doctor said I would be fine. One thing I will probably have though is black crap for a few days, due to the excessive iron intake, (tongue in cheek). I had to attend a meeting with the school, in which they fired quite a few questions at me. They came to the conclusion that I could go back to my old class, if I promised to attend school. I said that I will try, so it was decided, I could re-join my friends.

The next day I got ready to go to school, I still didn't want to go, but managed to force myself. I walked into the classroom and saw Andy, one of my two friends, so I went and sat next to him. I asked him where Paul was, and he said they have moved him to another class. My first thought was of an angry nature, "They said I can go back to my old class with my friends", now they have moved one of them to accommodate me.

I did feel guilty that now because I'm back, they have penalised Paul. When I saw Paul at break time, I said to him that I had no idea he was going to be removed. He said that he didn't really mind, and quite likes his new class, so that made me feel a bit better. I was still struggling to attend school, but it was slightly better than before, I would go in for a couple of days, then have a day off.

This went on day after day, week after week, and month after month. I think the school ended up writing me off. I started to hang around with the wrong people, one lad in particular. I won't name this person, as he sadly passed away a long time ago, through drugs overdose, in this book I will refer to him as Bill. We could not go out anywhere, without getting into trouble in one way or another.

One particular time that I can recall, there were four of us and Bill suggested that we stay out all night. We said to him that our parents would never allow us out all night, so he said he had a plan. We were all to ask our parents if we can have a sleepover, and say it would be around each of our houses, we all agreed and went home to ask. The plan worked, so we all met around 9pm over by the lakes.

We all hoped our parents wouldn't check up on us, by phoning one of the other parents to see if we were actually staying there. It was summer time, so it was still light at this time. We didn't have any money, apart from a bit of loose change between us all. Bill then said if we wait until it was dark, we would go to a brewery that was nearby to steal some beer.

We were all a bit reluctant, but went along with the idea, so we waited until it was dark, made our way to the brewery, which was around a mile away. When we arrived, we saw several pallets of beer stacked up behind a tall wire fence. There were a couple of workers in there going about their business, they must be on a night shift. How were we going to climb the eight-foot fence, dodge the workers, and get back over the fence with a crate of beer?

This started to look like a stupid idea, until Bill said that the workers will probably have a tea break at some point, then we will make a move. Bill started to pull at the bottom of the fence, the workers were quite far away to hear anything, plus they couldn't see us as it was dark. Bill managed to pull the fence up just enough for someone to squeeze through. Now we had to decide who was going through to grab the beer. The other three were a bit older than me and a fair bit bigger, so I said I would do it.

We must have waited around twenty minutes when we saw the workers go through a door, now was my chance. Bill pulled up the fence, and I squeezed under, I just managed to wriggle myself through. Now I'm up on my feet, it was about seventy meters to the crates, I ran as fast as I could towards the beer. I grabbed a case of twenty-four cans then started to run back then I hesitated. If I can manage one case, why not two, so I turned back to grab another one.

Now, I was waddling back with two crates and struggling. I was almost there, where Bill was holding the fence up, then someone shouted "HEY YOU THERE, STOP". It was one of the workers, who had come back out of the door. So for the rest of the way I waddled as fast as I could, I just managed to reach the fence without dropping the crates.

At this point I was panicking, as the shouting was getting louder, I dropped the beer where Bill was holding up the fence. I said hurry up Bill, he pulled the crates through, then shouted at me to quickly crawl through. I didn't look behind, as I knew the worker was very close. I fell to the floor and wiggled through that gap as fast as I could, but doing so my jumper got snagged on the wire fence. "SHIT" I struggled like mad to get free, which ripped my jumper, but I didn't care, as long as I can get free.

I pulled at my jumper as hard as I could, "YES" I was free, I was up on my feet, and we ran as fast as we could through the bushes, then across the fields. When we were far away enough, we stopped, then Bill and I realised that we were well ahead of the other two who were carrying the beer.

When we finally got our breaths back, and saw the other two struggling with the crates, we burst out laughing. We all sat down and opened a can each, which exploded all over us, as they had been vigorously shaken up, then we lit up a cigarette each, they all patted me on the back, and told me they thought I was mad for grabbing two crates. We sat there for a while and drank a few more cans, which soaked us upon opening them every time.

I probably only had two to three cans, and was feeling a bit drunk, bearing in mind that I was only 11 at the time. We were running low on cigarettes, so Bill suggested looking in parked cars to see if someone left a pack in there, so that was our next mission. We tried quite a few cars, but we were out of luck, apart from a bit of loose change that we collected. We must have been trying the cars for a few hours, when all of a sudden a police car pulled up and told us all to freeze.

At the time, we were walking through a patch of long grass, so, I just dropped to the floor, hoping that the police didn't see me. I think I would have got away with it, if it weren't for Bill tripping over me. So, we all walked over to the police, and they said someone had phoned them regarding four lads breaking into cars, and we fit that description. So they made us get into their car and asked for our addresses, then they took us home.

As you can imagine, my mum was not too pleased receiving a knock on the door at 1am in the morning, to find me standing there, with a policeman on either side. That was just one instance, as I said earlier, we were either breaking into cars, or shops, or doing something that would get us into trouble.

I was not going to name my sister in this book, but I think you can make her name out in the paper clippings. She doesn't know I'm writing this, and I'm not sure if she would appreciate her name being mentioned. But what the heck, if she reads this book, I will have to pay the consequences if or when the time comes, Julie (sorry sis) is getting married. Her husband to be is her childhood sweetheart, Kevin, yes it's the same spotty (sorry Kev) 17 years old that got us out of the house on that fateful day.

My relationship with Julie is a lot better now that we are a bit older, but don't get me wrong, we still do have the odd fight, but now I'm getting older, I can stick up for myself a bit more. She was a bit more protective of me now, I think it was because she felt a bit guilty for what she put me through when I was younger.

One of the reasons I think she couldn't wait to move out was her relationship with mum's husband, Dick. They were constantly clashing, to the point where she had to move out for a while and rent a room. I can remember going to my nan's flat with mum and Dick one evening, the next thing Julie turned up there. Julie and Dick started arguing over something, then Julie pulled out a pair of scissors and slashed Dick down the side of his face. My mum and nan were frantic, as the blood was dripping off his face and onto the floor.

The thing with Julie is, she's okay until someone upsets her, and Dick surely knew how to upset people. The gash on his face actually looked worse than it was, he didn't need to have stitches. Anyway, Julie got married and moved out into her own place.

Moving again

We ended up moving again when I was 13, this was probably a good thing, as it got me away from hanging around with Bill and his friends. This place was around ten miles away. I said that I'm not moving schools again, so it was decided that I would stay at the same school. Dick used to drive me there every day (the days I attended), I did say he was all right sometimes. Our new house was by the sea, with arcades and amusements, which I thought was great, I made some new friends who lived down my street, everything was looking good. I used to love it in the arcades, I would be in there for hours.

After living there for a few months, I started to get wise when to play the machines. I suppose you could say I was getting addicted to playing them, especially space invaders. I was obsessed with trying to beat the high score. I used to say to myself, 'I'm so close to that high score and I am going to beat it'. I would spend every penny I had on them, and if I didn't have the money, I would get it one way or another. It didn't take me long to beat that high score, the amount of time and money I spent on that machine I'm not surprised.

So I had the high score on space invaders, it stayed up there for around two weeks, then someone had beaten it by 500 points. I was absolutely gutted when I see that on the machine, I had to get my name back on top of the score board. I had no money on me, so went back home to ask my mum. My mum then said, that I had enough money yesterday, so I couldn't have anymore. I then left the house in a huff, it sounds like I was a spoilt little brat, but I wasn't really, I felt like I had to get that high score back, no matter what it took.

One day I found myself looking at my mum's purse when she was out of the room, and before I knew it, I was taking some loose change out and putting it in my pocket, which I'm very ashamed to admit. This went on for a while, I would take some change from my mums purse, then spend it on the machines. One particular day my friends and I planned on having a day out, to a place called Southend On Sea, which is around ten miles away from where we lived. This was in 1978, so £2 would have been plenty of money for a day out.

I shamefully took a £5 note from my mum's purse, so I now had £7 what with the £2 my mum already gave me. What a day out we all had, I was buying food and sweets for everyone, paying for rides in the fun fair, I was on a high. This felt like I was on some sort of drug, and what an adrenaline rush I had. When I got home, I started to feel a bit low. It felt like I was coming down from being high on a drug, that's the only way I can describe it, I wanted that rush of adrenaline back.

Taking money from my mums purse started to escalate, the £5 turned to £10, the £10 turned to £20, I couldn't stop myself. I was taking my friends for days out, even offering to buy them clothes. My mum had an idea that I was taking money, as she used to hide her purse, why didn't she say something to me.

One day I went too far, Dick had just come home, after drawing some money out from the bank, he hung his coat up then went into the kitchen. I walked passed his coat and noticed an envelope sticking out of the pocket. I peered in and saw a few £20 notes, I left them there, then went upstairs. I sat on my bed for a while, I was feeling nervous, and I had butterflies in my stomach.

Then I stood up and went downstairs, Dick and my mum were now in the garden. I went to his coat, took out the envelope and put the cash in my pocket. I then opened the front door and discarded the envelope under his car, then went back upstairs and locked myself in the bathroom. I reached into my pocket and took out the bundle of notes, and started to count it.

Oh my god, there was £140, that was a lot of money back then. I then went into my bedroom, where I hid the wad of cash. It must have been an hour or so later, when I heard raised voices downstairs. I could hear Dick saying, "I definitely put the envelope in my coat pocket". I started to feel very guilty at what I had done, but the thought of that high and adrenaline rush I had on that day out, outweighed the feeling of guilt.

I then heard the front door go, so I looked out of my bedroom window. I saw Dick approach his car, I then could see the envelope about three metres away from where I threw it. Dick must have spotted it as well, as he went over and picked it up. He was walking around the car, looking underneath and looking into the car, then he come back in. I could hear Dick speaking to my mum, I heard him say that the envelope must have dropped out of his pocket as he got out the car, and some lucky bastard has picked it up, taken the cash out, and dropped the envelope.

I still felt very bad for what I'd done, but at the same time felt a sense of achievement, I've managed to cover my tracks, they can't suspect me.

I left it for around a week to let the dust settle, then I made plans to have a day out in Southend again. I invited a couple of friends to join me, and told them they won't need any money. Wow what a day we had, we sat in a top restaurant, and ordered a three course meal, we went on all the rides at the fair ground, in which some we had around four rides. I bought clothes for myself and my friends, I was on cloud nine. At the time I was oblivious to what I had done, and how bad that was to steal from my own mum.

When I got home, I managed to hide the new clothes I had bought, I knew I couldn't wear them in front of mum, as she would want to know where they came from. I used to wear the clothes underneath my normal clothes, then change when I was out. Before long, all this was to come crashing in around me. A few days after my day out, my mum received a phone call from my friends mum. She asked my mum, if that was ok with her that I bought my friend the clothes. So I had been found out, she was pretty angry with me, but Dick went absolutely crazy, I don't blame him really, I think I would have done the same. Things did finally calm down, after I did a lot of grovelling.

So now I had no pocket money indefinitely (which I know I didn't deserve), and I was certainly not going to ask for any. I would go to the arcades to watch other people playing. In the summer time it used to get very busy at the seafront, and the penny pushing machines used to get very full. Sometimes money used to just fall out with no one playing them, so I would go around collecting this. Once I had enough, I would change it up at the cashier's desk, then I would go and play space invaders.

I heard through the grapevine that, if you put a small elastic band around a ten pence piece, then put it in the fifty pence change slot in the fruit machines, it will pay-out five-ten pence pieces. So I thought I would give this a go. The next day I walked to the shops to buy a bag of elastic bands. They had to be small enough to stretch around a ten pence piece. After going into a couple of shops, I managed to find the right size. I had three ten pence coins in my pocket, so off I went to the arcades.

Before I arrived, I opened the elastic bands and stretched one around a coin. I walked over to one of the fruit machines that was not in view of the change kiosk, Ok, let's see if this works. I pulled out the coin and put it in the change slot, I heard the machine swallow the coin, then heard the sound of coins hitting the metal tray. "YES", it's only bloody worked. I quickly fiddled around with another coin and elastic band, and put that one in, "YES" it's worked again.

I've put twenty pence in and got £1 back, brilliant. But then I thought I have got to be careful here, I don't want to bring any attention to myself. There was around five different arcades, so I went in all of them and done this little trick twice, and had the same result, I spent £1 and had £5 back. My pockets were quite full, fifty ten pence pieces is quite a lot of change to carry around. I then thought that I would go back home, have my dinner, then I would go back there later on.

So that evening, I put my coat on with deep pockets, made sure I had my elastic bands, and left for the arcades. I targeted one machine that was in the corner and was out of the way. I had already made up a pocket full of coins with bands around them, so started feeding them in. I knew that I probably will only have one chance at this, as when the people that worked there emptied the machines, instead of coins, they will find a load of elastic bands.

It didn't take long before my pockets were bulging with coins, and I could not fit anymore in. I had a couple of carrier bags that I bought with me, so I left the arcade and went around the back. It was dark so no one could see, I sat on a bench and made up another load of coins with the bands. Then I filled one of the bags I had with the rest of the coins, then I hid the bag in a bush.

Once I was satisfied that no one could see it, I made my way to a different arcade. Again I targeted a machine that was out of the way, and started feeding the coins in. After a while of filling my pockets, I thought there was something wrong with the machine, it was making a noise as if the change was coming out, but there was no coins. I then realised that I had cleared the machine out.

When I went to leave, I realised I must have more coins this time, as my pockets seemed a lot heavier. I tried not to look to conspicuous whilst I was walking, which was difficult considering the amount of coins I had in my pockets, I collected the bag I hid, then made my way home. I was glad to arrive back without the bag splitting, good job they were strong carrier bags. My mum was in the lounge watching TV, so I shouted out that I was home, then rushed up stairs. I emptied my pockets, and the bag onto my bedroom floor, and began counting it out. I couldn't believe it, £58.50 in ten pence pieces. I went downstairs and began telling my mum what I done, and that I wanted to give it to her, towards what I had taken. She was annoyed at what I had done, but said that was a nice gesture anyway. She then said for me to keep the money, as long as I promise not to do it again.

Next time I went to the arcades, I noticed that all the change slots on the fruit machines had a screw in them, so no one could use the slots, I wonder why?

Marathon man

A couple of years have passed, I'm now 15 years old, my nan came to live with us due to an accident that she had. She had a fall and broke her hip, plus my nan had cataracts so had limited vision. She had the downstairs spare bedroom, which was perfect for her, as she was in a wheelchair for a while. I had about six months to go before I officially left school, when I found a job in a clothing factory.

This job was around three miles from where I lived, so I used my bicycle as a means of transport. I only lasted for around three weeks, as I didn't like it, so I left. I never returned to school for the last six months, and the school never contacted me. So here I am, no qualifications, no job, I didn't really know what I wanted to do. One day my brother-in-law (Kev) asked me if I wanted to go for a run with him, he used to keep himself fit at the time. I wasn't interested in running as I hated doing that in PE at school. But I thought, what the heck it's something to do I suppose.

He came over to pick me up in his car, then we left and drove to a place where he always run. This place was a hilly six mile loop around a country park. We arrived at the car park, then got out and Kev began to do some stretching. I just stood there flapping my arms around like a demented duck, the only stretching I had done before was in the morning when I got out of bed, by lifting my arms above my head and yawning.

After around ten minutes we were ready to go. So off we went, the first mile or two felt really easy, bearing in mind the only running I had done before was cross country at school. Mile three Kev started to pick up the pace and had a four metre gap on me, so I responded with a quick burst of pace to get back on his shoulder. I then saw the look on Kev's face, it was the look of surprise, and he was thinking, "You shouldn't be able to keep up with me at this pace". I was still finding this pace quite easy, so I carried on running alongside him for five minutes.

Kev's breathing started to become quite laboured, so I started to chat to him, saying, "do you want to pick the pace up slightly Kev?, in which he replied with a laboured grunt, "no" so that was my cue to pick the pace up slightly. Kev did not respond to the injection of pace, I could hear him behind me, which I can only describe as a dying buffalo.

I didn't look behind me, I knew Kev was dropping further back because the grunts we're getting fainter. At this point I was feeling really good, I was buzzing, so I increased the pace in further. I had about a mile to go, which was mainly up a steep hill. I was pushing myself hard on the last mile; I just looked at the ground, and pumped my arms all the way up the hill until I arrived back at the car park. It took me around thirty seconds to recover, then I was breathing normally. Kev arrived back a couple of minutes behind me, then five minutes later when he recovered, he said to me, "you need to join a running club".

I finally found something that I was good at, never in a million years would I have thought it would be running. I didn't like it in school, although I must have been fairly good at it, because the teachers would always pick me for the cross country team. That run I had with Kev had changed my mind about running, I enjoyed it. The next day I found out where the local running club was, this was called Canvey Athletic Club which was about 1.5 miles away.

They trained on Tuesday and Thursday evenings, so I went down on my bike, where I met the coach who introduced himself as Ernie. He asked me what my preferred distance was, in which I replied long distance, I knew I was never going to be a sprinter, I wanted to do long distance road races. So Ernie said the training session for that evening was going to be 4x800 metre reps. Well, that session felt fast, I was not used to running quick, in fact I was not used to running any sort of pace. I think I did ok though, there was a group of around eight runners, a couple were around my age, while the rest were a lot older.

I was finishing the reps in second or third place, with the ones in front being older and more experienced. After the session the coach said that I done exceptionally well, considering that was my first session. We warmed down and stretched, then I hopped on my bike and rode home. I felt quite pleased with myself, with a sense of achievement, and I was looking forward to the next training night. I started to train most days, where I would go out on my own and run anything from 6 to 18 miles.

I remember one time I woke up at around 3:30am and couldn't go back to sleep. I thought I might as well go out for my run now, as I'm laying here and I can't sleep, it will save doing it later. So off I went on a 12 mile run at 4am, I bet people that drove past me must have thought I was mad at that time in the morning. I entered myself into a few small races e.g. 5 to10k, but always found them too quick for me personally. I wanted to run half and full marathons, like I said the longer the better. I was actually too young to run a full marathon as you have to be eighteen, but my coach said I could run one but it will have to be unofficial, so I said that would be fine.

So he entered me into the Bristol Marathon, I didn't know at the time, but this course was one of the hilliest in Britain (I'm only 15, thanks Ernie). There were other runners from the club that had entered into this race, so I travelled with them. This was around 3.5 hour's trip from where I lived, so we left at 5:30am for a 10:00am race start time.

We arrived around 8:50am, just enough time to get parked and to warmed-up before the start. I started to get slightly nervous about ten minutes before the race, and I was thinking what have I let myself in for. It was a fairly warm day if I remember rightly, and I was standing on the start line along with nearly 800 other athletes, oblivious to what lied ahead. The gun went off and all I could hear was 1,600 running shoes hitting the road.

I'm thinking what am I going to feel like after mile 18, as that's the furthest I have run in a training session. I quickly got that thought out of my head, and said to myself 'just concentrate on a mile at a time'. The first mile was quite flat, apart from a few little inclines. However this was short lived, as the second and third mile I would have been better off with a pair of mountain boots. I was thinking that I hope it's not this hilly for the whole course. The 4th and 5th mile wasn't too bad, then I had mile 5. That just got steeper and steeper as it went on, it was relentless.

Mile six, "YES", a much-welcomed water station, as I said it was a fairly warm day, especially for running 26.2 miles. I approached the stretched out arm that was holding the cup of water, I went to grab it but missed. I had a second attempt at another arm holding a sponge, "YES", got it. I was desperate for a drink, so I ended up sucking the water from the sponge, it didn't taste that great, but I didn't care at the time, as long as it was cold and wet.

Now I had to wait until mile 12 for the next water station, so I tried to get as much water out of that sponge as possible. I don't know what happened, but next I was approaching mile 11, and I can't recall miles seven to ten, I must have switched off.

This was another killer mile, and it took its toll, I was thinking how can I finish this race, I'm not even half way yet, I had to dig deep.

Mile 12 was like an oasis, my mouth was so dry that I couldn't even spit. There were the outstretched arms with that lovely cold water, and sponges. I said to myself, "You better not miss this one". As I approached the water, I grabbed it and this time I got it, then with my other hand I grabbed a sponge. I didn't realise how hard it was to drink and run at the same time, most of the water was going up my nose and around my face. I squeezed the sponge on top of my head and on the back of my neck, the cold water was absolute bliss.

A few more miles passed, some had killer hills and some didn't, and I was fast approaching mile 18. This was where I thought that once I pass this I'm in no man's land, but then there was another water station there, so that took my mind off it a bit. I managed to grab another drink and sponge, this time the drink went over my head, and I drank from the sponge. I found this easier to do, and I could hold on to the sponge and suck it. So now I was in no man's land and I wasn't feeling too bad at this point. Two more miles had passed, so now I've got 20 miles behind me, just another 6.2 in front.

Mile 22, "OH MY GOD", I had well and truly hit the wall, my legs had turned to lead, I could barely lift my arms, and my head felt like it was going to explode because it was so hot. How am I going to finish the last 4 miles, I cannot move my legs, it felt like I was running through water that was up to my waist. And to top it all off the next mile was another one where I needed mountain boots, I think I walked a part of that one. I had three miles to go, which was approximately 20 minutes of running left to do.

I managed to get to the top of the hill and start running again, I still felt like I was running in water, I started to doubt myself that I would be able to finish at this point. Then I heard a little voice in my head say, "Stop complaining and concentrate, you can do a lot more than you could ever imagine". This was like a light bulb come on in my head, then I put my head down and drove on, all the time I was repeating in my head, "You can do a lot more than you could ever imagine".

Mile 24, another welcomed water station, but I felt a bit fresher than I did before, I think I had my second wind. I was at mile twenty-five, and it was at a top of a hill, I could see the crowds of spectators in the distance, and I knew that was the finish. I'm saying to myself, "C'mon Clive you can do it", I've only got one mile to go, c'mon dig deep. I ran down the hill which was about four hundred metres, the rest of the way was a slight incline. Half a mile to go and I'm digging deep, the spectators that lined the streets were cheering and clapping as I ran passed them, I think it was the spectators that took me to the finish line on that day.

I came 24th out of almost 800 athletes in 3 hours exactly, not bad at 15 for my first marathon.

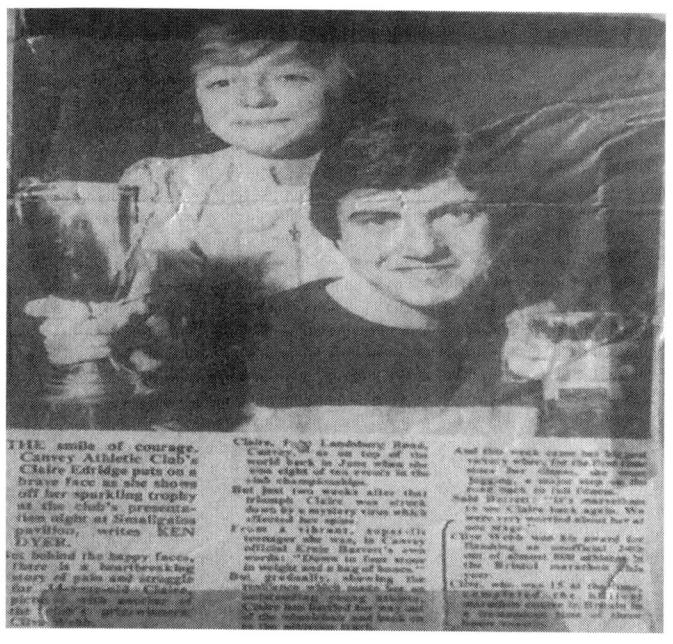

The next day I couldn't walk, it took me about three days before I could run properly again, my legs felt like they had been run over by a steamroller. My nan had now been living with us for around six months and her cataracts were really affecting her eyesight. I would go into the lounge where she would be sitting, and she would say, "Is that you Clive".

She could see things a lot better when they were close up, but anything that was six feet or more away, was quite blurry. My nan never ate anything after her dinner, which would be around 5pm. But on this particular night around 10pm she asked my mum for some toast. She said she felt quite hungry, so mum made two slices of toast. Then she said goodnight to everyone and went to bed.

The next morning when she saw my mum, she asked her if she had an argument with Dick in the early hours. Bearing in mind mum and Dick frequently argued over money or over me. My mum said that she hadn't had an argument, and asked my nan what brought about the question. Then nan said, in the early hours, her bedroom door came open and she saw a woman's figure standing there with her hand on her forehead.

What with my nan's eyesight being limited, she thought the figure was my mum holding her head, then thought she must have had an argument with Dick. Nan said the door came open, this figure was standing there holding her head, naturally, nan thought it was my mum and said, "What's the matter, have you had an argument". My nan then said as soon as she said that, the figure had gone.

The very next night, again this was around 10pm, nan asked for some toast which mum made her two slices. Nan ate the toast, then said she felt ravenous, could she have another two slices. She sat in the kitchen and ate another two slices while mum was standing at the sink washing up. Soon as nan finished eating, she said to mum that she had a sharp pain in her head. My mum then turned around to face her, and saw nan clutching her head, she then let out a cry, made a sort of gurgling noise, and died in front of my mum.

After the post mortem, it was revealed that my nan died of a massive brain haemorrhage. What did my nan see the night before she died? This is something else that I cannot explain. I was out with some friends when my nan passed away, I came home around 30 minutes later. I took her death pretty bad, and didn't want to speak to anyone for a long time after. My grieving reflected in my training, I suppose you could say it was in a good way. I felt angry with myself that I wasn't there for my nan when she passed. I was too busy having a good time with my friends. So I would pull my running shoes on and take my anger out on the roads.

One session I can remember was a ten-mile run, which was an out and back route from my house, with a 1.5 mile very steep hill at the halfway point, I had no stopwatch, it was me against myself. I stretched for around 15 minutes before I set off around 7pm. The first couple of miles felt too easy, so I picked the pace up. I was feeling really good, although I knew I was going at a fair pace at this point. So I upped the ante again with another injection of pace.

I was at the 3.5-mile mark and at the bottom of the steep hill. I started running up the hill, and it felt like I was going faster as the hill got steeper. I've never felt like this before, I'm normally breathing a lot harder than this going up that hill. When I reached the top my breathing was normal, it was like I was walking. That was five mile and the halfway point, then I turned around and just let myself go down the hill.

I was letting gravity do the work, but I thought I must be careful here as to not lose my balance. I was thinking, I needed to concentrate as there were a few potholes, but something took over my vision, because I wasn't even looking down at the ground. I seemed to know where the holes were, as I was leaping over them without looking. I got to the bottom of the hill where the ground levelled out, and it seemed like my pace stayed the same on the flat as it was coming down the hill. I obviously was not sprinting, but that's what it felt like, all the way back home felt like I kept picking the pace up, and when I arrived home I wasn't even breathing very hard. I wish they invented GPS watches back then, as I think I ran a pretty decent time for a 10 miler.

My running club was to host the first Canvey Marathon, which I thought was great, I can run a marathon on my home turf. I had around two months to prepare for this, so I didn't have a great deal of time. Training didn't go that well for the two months, as I picked up a slight knee injury which put me out for three weeks. Then I picked up a cold which lasted a few days a week before the race, but I made it to the start line. It was quite windy on the day, which was going to be a problem along the seafront.

I lived on Canvey Island, which is what it says on the tin, 'an Island'. Canvey is a little over eight miles in radius, so the course consisted of three laps around Canvey, then about a mile loop of a holiday park, which took you straight past the finish, which proved to be a bit soul destroying.

I had quite a few spectators that knew me out on the course, plus a few I didn't know. There was a bit of a write-up in the local paper about a young Canvey lad who was only 16 running. It was fairly rare back then for someone so young running a marathon. There must have been around 700 athletes on the start line and I started to feel cold in the wind whilst waiting for the gun to go off, although I had a tee shirt on under my vest.

Finally the gun fired and we were off, Steve from my club was going to lead the front runners around for the first mile, as there were quite a few left and right turns. I think there were about 15 runners in the lead group, and I was in the second group of around 10.

We were approaching the first mile just before we hit the sea front, the lead group was about 30 meters in front of us when I saw Steve drop out. Steve was a year older than me, and had been running a lot longer, but he didn't want to attempt the marathon, He probably had more sense. As I ran past him I shouted out, "LIGHTWEIGHT" with a smile on my face, to which he replied with a smile back, and a few words of encouragement.

A couple of minutes later we hit the seafront, No I need to rephrase that, the seafront hit us. The wind was so strong that we were barely moving, all I could do was try to tuck myself in behind the other runners, and use them as a windshield. We had around 3 miles of battling the wind along the seafront before we turned right. That was tough, and it took the wind out of my sails, pardon the pun. My group started to split up as a couple pushed on in front, but most of them started to drop back.

We were fast approaching the first lap, and my group was down to just two, me and a guy in his 30s. I wasn't feeling too good and started to doubt myself if I could finish, I knew I wasn't 100% before I started, and now I'm thinking was this wise for me to have turned up today. My pace started to slow, and the guy moved a couple of metres in front of me. My breathing was becoming increasingly laboured, then instead of gaining a bigger gap on me, this guy that I was running with slowed down until I was level with him.

He asked if I was ok, and I replied, "no I'm really suffering". He then said to dig in and that feeling will pass, so I carried on relentless. That spurred me on for a couple of miles, but then come the seafront for the second time. This was like running in a wind tunnel, my legs were moving, but I wasn't going anywhere. I had to stop, I had nothing left, the guy then stopped with me. I told him that I think I'm going to drop out, and said for him to carry on. He then said he would walk with me until I recover, so we walked for about 15 seconds, but I was feeling bad for him as he was sacrificing his own race, so I said, ok let's carry on.

We battled with the wind for another 3 miles along the seafront, and I was also battling with my thoughts of quitting. Again we were approaching the two lap point, and I told the guy to leave me and carry on, and I stopped. He then stopped with me and began to jump around holding his hamstring muscle. I thought, "What is this guy doing", he then said that every time that he stops, it's causing him to have cramp in his hamstring. I knew that this was a ploy to keep me running. This guy was a complete stranger, yet he was going to all these lengths to help me finish.

So I tried to carry on yet again, I'm thinking there's no way I can run another mile let alone another lap. I managed to make the seafront and although I just wanted to drop out, the wind had died down a little bit. The guy kept looking around to see if I was still there, and I just tried to stick on his shoulder, if I started to drop off, he would slow up and give me a few words of encouragement. We made it to the other end of the seafront for the last time, we had a little over 5 miles to the finish.

I was just about to stop again, but this time, I think I would have dropped out completely. Then I remembered that voice I heard in my head in the last marathon. So I kept thinking to myself, 'stop complaining and concentrate, you can do a lot more than you could ever imagine'. So I battled on relentlessly until we made it to the holiday park, yes I could see the finish about 800 meters away. I dragged myself along for the last 800, then I could have actually cried when I realised that we had an extra mile to do around the holiday park. I don't know how I managed to get around that holiday park, but I did, as we approached the finish line the guy slowed up so I crossed the line in front of him.

My family was there at the finish to greet me, but I was pretty spaced out to acknowledge them. All I could do as I stood there with this guy was shake his hand and thank him for what he had done, and I said I would not have finished that race if it weren't for him. Our times and positions in this marathon were, 2 hours and 47 minutes, 18th, and 19th respectively. Who knows what time and position this guy could have achieved, if he just left me, and run his own race. There is more to this particular story that I will tell later on the book.

Please excuse the photos being so blurry

Along the seafront

Not too much to say about the next race apart from that I was still 16, and this race was the Essex county 5k road championship. There were around 25 athletes in this race, and I finished 3rd and won a bronze medal.

Clive Webb *Little boy lost*

A couple of years have now passed, I'm 18 now, and I have passed my driving test. My mum bought me my first car, this was a surprise, and I had no idea that they had planned this. So now I'm mobile, great I haven't got to rely on people giving me lifts everywhere. One day I went to visit my nan's grave to lay some flowers. She only had a homemade cross with her name on it, then I had an idea. I'm going to build a brick surrounding with four small piers on each corner.

So I went back home and mentioned this idea to my mum. She thought it was a great idea, so I said I would work out what materials I would need, then take a trip to the builder's merchant. I then sat down and made a list of everything that I would need. The surrounding was going to be two brick courses high, with four piers at four courses high.

So I worked out how many bricks I needed, sand, cement, and ballast for the footing.

I already had a trowel and a shovel, so off I went to buy the materials. I had to make a couple of trips, as I couldn't fit it all in my little ford escort. I just about made it home with the car axels nearly touching the floor, good job a police car didn't pass me. So now I had all the materials at home, and I needed to go and dig the footing. It didn't need to be that deep as it's only going to be a couple of courses high.

Once I dug the footing, I went back home to pick up the ballast and cement. Then I thought, how am I going to mix the concrete, there was now here in the graveyard that I could do it.

So then I had another idea, I will mix it at home, then load my car boot up with it. So I pulled out the carpet from my boot, mixed the concrete, and loaded my boot. I had a couple of buckets to transport the concrete from the car to the grave, so I put them on my back seat, and off I went. It was hard work waddling to the grave with two buckets of concrete at a time, I had around 150 metres from my car to the grave.

Finally, the last two buckets were poured in, and my arms were really aching by now. So I levelled off the concrete then made my way home. The next day I took the bricks to the graveyard, then I went back home to mix the mortar. I did the same as I did with the concrete, and built the surrounding. I was just clearing up when someone from the church came over and said to me that I will have to take the surrounding down.

I must say, I didn't take that very well. I said to the guy that we have paid for our plot, what was the problem? There was no way I'm taking it down. He then said if I didn't do it, then the church would. So I said to him that he must do what he had to do, but there was no way I was taking it down, and I left it like that. That surrounding is still standing to this day, 35 years later.

A job offer came up with Kev's brother (Dave), this was roof tiling. I found this a tough job to do, although I was extremely fit, I was a very slim 18-year-old. Dave had a lot of character, and had the same sense of humour as me. My first-day roofing was back breaking, it took me quite a long time to get used to this new job. My training suffered dramatically for a few months, as I was just too tired to go for a run when I got home in the evening.

Eventually, I started to get back into running again, and decided to enter into the Basildon Marathon, this again was organised by my running club. I won't go into details about this race, as I don't want to bore you with yet another marathon. But what I will say is, half way through this race I was in a group of around eight athletes, and a marshal sent us the wrong way. We actually ended up running an extra half a mile.

Holiday mode

Dave and I were becoming good friends, we were working together and meeting up for drinks after work. One day we decided to book a holiday and after much debate, we booked a week on the Greek Island of Corfu. This was a late booking and only had three days until we fly. So it was a bit of a rush to get things sorted, but what do two single blokes need for a week, apart from a few pairs of shorts, and half a dozen t-shirts.

Dave is 6 years older than I am so he must have been 24 at the time, Kev gave us a lift to the airport, so we were off. This was my first holiday without my family, I was quite excited. We had a 30-minute coach journey from the airport to our hotel. Once we checked in and threw our cases in our room, we headed for the bar. We sunk a few beers, and started to feel hungry, so headed out to the main strip for a bite to eat, and one or ten more beers. We had a good night trying out a bit of local cuisine and sampling a beer or two in most of the bars. All seemed fine for a couple of days. We tried out water skiing which we were absolutely useless at, had a trip to the next town to see what that was like. Then we decided to book a trip to the mainland, which was a ferry crossing.

On the way over, everything was fine, we had a bite to eat, had a look around, all the usual stuff. It was on the way back that things started to go wrong. We must have been a couple of miles out at sea, and we were sitting on the top deck. We were chatting to a couple of girls that we met, and everything seemed fine. We were sitting at a table that was right beside the guard rail on the side of the ferry. Then out of the blue Dave said, "I think I've worked it out, but I'm not sure".

Then he climbed on top of the guard rail, and jumped straight off the top of the ferry and into the sea. I couldn't believe what I had just seen, I quickly looked over the side to see Dave hit the water. The water was very rough that day and all I could see was his head appearing then disappearing between the waves in the water, he looked like a little peanut bobbing up and down.

There was panic on the upper deck, everyone started shouting, I then heard someone shout, "MAN OVER BOARD". The ferry then started sounding the horn, then slowly stopped, and began to reverse back to where Dave was in the water. At this point no one could see where Dave was, the water was so rough that it was literally like trying to spot a peanut bobbing up and down in the water. People were hanging over the side trying to find him, they were running from one side of the ferry to the other, in a hope of spotting Dave.

Then a horrible thought came over me, and I think this same thought was in the minds of everyone else on that ferry, had he drowned. The ferry was still sounding its horn and the shouting and screaming started to die down. It was like all the noise was winding down, a bit like a clockwork toy running out of its wind. Then there was an eerie silence, which seemed like it went on for ages, but was probably only a minute or so. Then someone screamed, "THERE HE IS", and was pointing to a section of the water to the left-hand side of the rear of the ferry.

Then I could just about see his head bobbing up and down, so the ferry reversed as close as it could and the crew pulled him on board. Once he was checked over to see if he was alright, the captain said he would have to spend the rest of the journey below deck. All this time I'm thinking Dave has done this just for the fun of it. The captain wanted to speak to me to ask what happened. I told him that Dave slipped through the guard rail by accident, I said that we had been drinking for most of the day, and I think Dave just lost his balance.

    The captain said ok, but Dave must still remain down below for the rest of the journey. He then said he cannot take any chances as he is responsible for the well-being of all the passengers on board. He also added that if this incident had been worse, he could have been looking at 20 years in prison under Greek law. When he put it like that, I didn't blame him for keeping Dave away from the upper deck. It wasn't long before we were back, then I asked Dave, did he jump just for the fun of it, he didn't say a word, but just gave me a blank stare.

Things didn't stop there, it was the day we were due to come home, then Dave went missing. I woke up at 7.30am, and noticed that Dave wasn't in his bed. We had to be out of our room by 9am, and the coach was due to pick us up at 12pm and take us to the airport. I got dressed and went down to see if Dave was having breakfast. But he wasn't in the restaurant, so I looked around the hotel, but there was no sign of him. I sat and had my breakfast in the hope that he would show up.

I thought to myself, I better go back to the room and start packing, thinking Dave will probably show up then. I packed all my things, and there was still was no sign of Dave, so I packed his things in his case. It was now fast approaching 9am, so I double checked the room to make sure I packed everything then made my way to the reception. I sat in the lobby for around an hour and there was still no sign of him.

By this time I started to panic, and I'm thinking, where the fuck is he. I gave it another 30 minutes, then I went to the receptionist to report Dave missing. She was very helpful, and got straight on the telephone and rang the local hospital. She gave them his name and a description, but they said they hadn't had any English patients in for a couple of days. Then the receptionist phoned the police station, but had no luck there.

By now we only had about an hour before the coach was due to arrive, and I was thinking to myself that I couldn't just leave without him, I will have to miss the flight home until he was found. It was 11.45am when Dave strolled into the reception, and he looked terrible, all he had on was a pair of shorts and a t-shirt. He was barefoot and covered in mud. I said to him, "DAVE, WHERE THE FUCK

HAVE YOU BEEN?" in which he replied, "you know where I've been, sitting up on the hill".

This hill was about a mile away from our hotel, I then said not to worry about it now, you have got about 10 minutes to get cleaned up and have a change of clothes. I asked the receptionist if it would be possible to have our keys back, so Dave could get changed. She said that would be fine as the new holidaymakers had not arrived yet. So we went back to the room and Dave had a quick shower and had a change of clothes.

When we went back down to the reception, the coach was just pulling into the car park. We made it to the airport and onto the plane, once we were airborne Dave started to get restless. He said to me that he wanted to get off the plane, then left his seat and headed for the door. I immediately followed him and was asking him to return to his seat. He would not listen and continued to make his way to the aircraft's door.

Some of the other passengers began to notice, and they were looking very uneasy. There was an air hostess standing in front of the door, who then asked Dave if she could help him, to which he replied that he needed to get off the plane. The hostess looked quite worried at that point, then asked Dave to return to his seat. He then tried to push past her in an attempt to grab the door handle. I then said to her that Dave had been drinking (but he hadn't), and not to worry as I will deal with the situation.

I then calmed Dave down and said to him that we were nearly home, where his brother (Kev) would be waiting for us. He seemed to listen to what I had just said, then agreed to return to his seat. That flight seemed to last forever, I was constantly on tender hooks wondering what Dave was going to do next. When we finally landed, I let out a big sigh of relief. When we finally collected our cases and was heading towards the exit I saw Kev.

I have never been so happy to see a familiar face, he was oblivious to what was going on, but knew something was up by the look on my face. Kev asked us if we were ok, in which I replied, "NO WE ARE NOT OK". I briefly told him what was going on, and said Dave needs to get some help. I don't think Dave recognised Kev, and I don't think he actually knew where he was.

When we arrived at Kev's car, we put our suit cases in and got seated, Dave said to Kev, "take me to Benitses", that was a resort we visited in Corfu. When we arrived home, Dave got the help that he needed, and had a week in the hospital. The doctors said he had a breakdown that could have been brought on for a number of reasons.

A few months had passed, and I started to get bored with my job, then I had an idea. I'll start training really hard and I might be able to become an Olympian. So I left my job in the pursuit to become a top athlete. I started to train hard, but I wasn't training right. All I was doing was running, there was no structure to my training. I could not make out why my race times were not coming down, I thought that I should be beating these guys who were beating me.

I started to get disheartened, I'm training come rain or shine with no improvement. This went on for around a year, then I hung up my running shoes, and gave up. So now what am I going to do? I had no job, no money, I felt a bit lost. I then ended up working with Dave again, although this wasn't what I wanted to do, but in saying that, I didn't really know what I wanted to do. A couple of years had passed, and my 21st birthday was nearly upon me. Julie and Kev were booking a holiday to a Greek Island called Skiathos, and asked if I wanted to join them. I said yes I would love to come, so they booked the holiday. I would be celebrating my birthday out there which I thought was great. On the holiday I pretty much did my own thing, I went to the nightclubs by myself.

Before long I met a group of three Norwegian guys, and we got quite friendly. I used to meet up with them and we would go on bar crawls, we had such a laugh together. Funny thing was, on the night of my birthday, I met the guys in a bar. One guy (Roy) said it was his birthday, and he is 21, I wished him happy birthday, then I burst out laughing. When Roy asked what was so funny, I said to him that it's my birthday too, and I'm 21.

Then they all burst out laughing, and we said we would celebrate our birthdays together. WOW, what a celebration that was, it lasted for three days. I didn't know where we went, or how we got there. But what I can remember is being in a bar that was full of English and Scandinavians. I was sitting up at the bar with Roy next to me. All the people in the bar knew that we were celebrating our birthdays, so they egged us on to do a drinking competition, England v Norway.

I had a big group of English people gathered behind me, and Roy had the Norwegians behind him, LET THE GAMES BEGIN! We started downing pint after pint, as soon as we finished one, another was put in front of us. Good thing about it was we weren't paying for the drinks. If I downed one first, the Norge's bought us a drink, if Roy downed his first, the English did the same. Every time one of us won, our group that was gathered behind us would let out a loud cheer.

Roy and I kept looking at each other then burst out laughing, it was madness in that bar, but one happy memory. Next thing that I can remember on that three day bender (and there must be a lot that I can't remember) was being at a beach party. There was a guy there that kept rugby tackling everyone, as soon as someone went down to have a swim, BANG, they were flat out on the floor. He started to annoy people, as he didn't know when to stop.

He then started bragging on how good he was at everything, "you know the type of person I'm talking about, one that needs to be brought back down to earth". He then wanted to arm wrestle everyone or do anything that was a competition. My ears pricked up when I heard him say, "I bet no one here can beat me in a race to the end of the bay and back". Bearing in mind that I was still pretty fit at the time, I was still doing a bit of running, I just wasn't competing.

So I said to him that I might race him, but I think he will probably beat me as I'm not that good at running. He then replied, that I was probably right, but what if we put a bet on it. I can't remember how many drachma it was, but it was roughly £10 which was worth a lot more back in 1986. So I said that I didn't really want to race him, as that's a lot of money to lose.

Then he started laughing and said come on what's the matter with you, I said ok then let's do it. Everyone was watching as we made a line in the sand, and I looked over to the Norge's and the crowd that gathered and gave them a little wink. It was roughly a mile to the end of the bay and back, and by the size of this guy, I knew that he was going to struggle. One of the crowd counted down, three, two, one, go, this guy went off like he was in a 100-metre race, and I had a little chuckle to myself, he soon slowed down and I was on his shoulder.

We had only covered about 400 metres and he was struggling, his breathing was really laboured, so I started chatting with him. I was asking him questions, to try and get him to speak, but he just looked at me with a scared and worried look on his face. I said to him that I didn't realise that running was so easy, and did he fancy picking the pace up a bit, in which he replied with a couple of grunts in his foreign tongue, I never asked what country he was from. I then said to him that I needed to go to the toilet, as I've had a fair bit to drink, so I will see you at the finish.

Then I said goodbye, and waved my hand and I was off. As I approached the finish line that was scraped in the sand, everyone was cheering, and Roy handed me a bottle of beer. It must have been close to a minute later when the guy fell over the line, I was actually on my second bottle of beer. Once he recovered, he said that he had a pain in his leg, and that's why he had to go slow, (which no one believed), then he said that the £10 was going to make him a bit short of money for the rest of his holiday. Then he fumbled around in his pocket, then handed me a couple of notes. I then said that I would do a deal with him, and when he asked what, I said you can keep the money on one condition.

When he said what the condition was, I said "for the rest of the beach party can you SHUT THE FUCK UP", and stop annoying everyone. He then replied with another couple of grunts in his mother tongue then walked off, we never saw him after that. Day two of our celebration I said to the Norge's that I better go back and let Julie know that I'm ok. When I arrived at our apartment she wasn't there, so I left a note in my room to let her know that I'm with the Norge's. I didn't realise at the time that she wouldn't be able to read it, as I had locked my door and I took the key with me.

After going to every bar that we could physically manage to visit, we ended up in a seedy nightclub in a different resort. I ended up having a bit of an argument with a guy from Finland, I don't know what it was over, but before I knew it his friend showed up and started to get involved. They both started speaking fairly loud in their mother tongue, then all of a sudden one of the Finnish guys got pushed by someone behind them.

Then I could see who pushed him because standing behind them were my three Norge friends. They started shouting at one another in Scandinavian, then the Finnish guys left. I thanked my friends but said to them, "it was lucky for the Finnish guys that you showed up, as I was about to get angry". I can't remember anything after that night, all I can remember was waking up in the morning on a lounger on the Norge's balcony. Then I left to make my way back to my apartment.

When I got back and knocked on Julie's room door, she answered and said, "where the hell have you been, you've been missing for 3 days and I have been worried sick, I've even informed the police that you were missing". I then replied that I was sorry, but I did leave a note, which she then said, "how was I supposed to read that, when you had locked the door and taken the key with you". I then said, "oh yeah, I can see your point". By the end of the holiday, I didn't want to come home, I was seriously thinking about staying there and maybe getting a job. But Julie and Kev ended up talking me out of it. But what a great time I had with those three guys from Norway.

When I returned, I was in holiday mode for quite a while, all I wanted to do was PARTY. Just before I went to Skiathos, I started going out with a group of friends I hadn't been in contact with for a while. I said to them, "why don't we all book a holiday together for the following year". So that's what we did, we booked a week in Lloret-de-mar, which is the northeast of Spain. We all used to go to a nightclub called the Kings club, which is on a holiday park on Canvey. The very same holiday park where I finished the marathon five years previously. What great nights out we all had there, we used to practically live over there. It was literally 3 minutes' walk (or in most cases 10 minutes staggering distance) from where I lived, so it was nice and local, with no need for a taxi.

The only nights we weren't there was Monday's, (unless it was a bank holiday), Tuesday's, and Wednesday's. I used to drink a bit too much in there most of the time, I was always saying to my friends, "come on, what's the matter with you all, let's have another", I just didn't know when to stop. A few months went by, and our lads holiday was fast approaching. This was around the time I met May, she was in Kings with a group of her friends, they all lived in a place called Chadwell-St-Mary, which was about 12 miles away. She had just turned 19 when I was introduced to her by her friend, and we used to meet up in Kings most nights.

The night before the holiday we all met in Kings as per usual. When it closed at 2am I decided it would be a good idea to go for a swim, there was a lake that was on the holiday park, so in I went fully clothed. In the morning we all travelled to London, where we were to board a coach for a 24-hour journey to Lloret. I'm not going to go into any details about the holiday, as it was a normal week away with the lads, eat, drink and sleep, pretty much for a week.

When we arrived home I phoned May and arranged to meet. I suggested to her that maybe we could book a holiday for next year, which she thought was a good idea. We tried to book a couple of places, but they were all fully booked, we then decided that we would have two weeks in Acapulco. My relationship with Dick was becoming quite bad at this time, so I ended up moving in with May.

It must have been about 3 months before our holiday when I said to myself that this holiday is going to be a good one. I decided that I would get myself as fit as I possibly could, so I got back into running. At the time I had my own van and was working in London. I would normally arrive back home around 5.30pm, then go straight out for a run. People thought that I was mad and say, "why do you run so much, your job must keep you fit", and they were probably right, but it wasn't fit enough for me.

I would push myself on every run that I did, it had to be, longer or faster, you could say I was obsessed. On the day of our holiday, Kev took us to the airport. On arriving at terminal, Kev came in with us, and waited with us in the queue. He then spotted someone that he recognised a couple of places in front of us. It was a couple that he knew that lived just around the corner to him.

And it just happened that they are going to the same destination as us. So we got chatting with them, and not only were they going to the same place, their hotel was just behind ours, but that's not all, this guy is also a roofer. We said that we will meet up there for a drink, and proceeded through to departures.

On boarding the plane we got seated and sat opposite an older couple in their 50s. We got chatting with them and asked where they were from, talk about a small world, they were from the same town as my sister and Kev, so now there were two couples from the same town. What a long flight that was, 14 hours with a stop off in Orlando. We arrived at our hotel around 11.30pm and I was buzzing. We had a stroll along the main strip for a while, I wanted to hit the nightclubs, but May was feeling tired, so we called it a night.

The next night we met up with the couple we met at the airport (Paul & Lynne), and went to a bar that was opposite our hotel. The girls were drinking wine, while Paul and I were drinking beer. After a while, I suggested that we try some tequila slammers, the girls declined, but Paul said he was up for it. I don't know what the matter was with me, but I could not get drunk, no matter how hard I tried. It must have been 1am, May and Lynne had fallen asleep at the table, Paul and I were still drinking beer, followed by a slammer.

At 1.30am Paul had enough, I said to him, "you must be joking, I'm just getting started". I then said, why don't we take the girls back to the rooms, then go and hit the nightclubs, he then declined, much to my disappointment. We woke the girls, and while they were coming too, I sank another few slammers. As the holiday went on, we went on a few excursions, one in particular that was unforgettable was the high divers, these guys would dive from a120ft cliff into a small gap of about 20ft, with jagged rocks either side of them. The taxis and their drivers were unforgettable too, the taxis were beat up old VW Beatles, and the drivers were mad as hatters.

One day when we got in a taxi, we said where we wanted to go, he said, "OK, but would you like some Acapulco gold, or a Mexican boy", we said no thank you, just take us to where we want to go. Acapulco gold was marijuana, and Mexican boys was exactly that. We were on the beach one day, and I saw one of the funniest things I've ever seen. This local guy was walking along the beach begging, he was walking all twisted up, he looked severely disabled, he was also dumb as he was just grunting at people, but once he had enough money, he stood up straight, then walked normally up to a bar, and said clear as day, uno cerveza por favor.

Another funny thing was when May and I were having breakfast in the hotel restaurant one morning. The other couple we met (Tom & Mary) on the plane, were staying in our hotel. Tom came in and asked the waiter for a jug of milk, but the waiter couldn't understand him. So Tom decided to put two fingers on his head, then walk up and down mooing like a cow. The waiter then said, "aaaahsi", then went to get a jug of milk. Good job it was early in the morning, if it was later, Tom may have had a rump steak.

Anyway the holiday finally came to an end, and it was time to come home. On the day of our departure we were told our flight was delayed for 24 hours. They said that there was trouble with one of the plane's engines, and this airline company only had one aircraft. This was not what we wanted to hear, just before a 14 hour flight. The hotel gave us free meals, but we had to sleep in the lobby as our rooms were taken by the second group of holiday makers. We finally boarded the plane and we were on our way home. We had a fair bit of turbulence on the journey, but I fell asleep.

I must have felt a pain jolt, which made me wake up, when I looked out of the window, I saw tree tops zooming past. At that point, I thought we were about to crash, I turned to May with a worried look on my face and she said that we were about to land at Gatwick. We exchanged telephone numbers with Paul and Lynne, and said we will meet up. Well that was a great holiday, but now it's back to the grindstone I suppose. This was the late 80s and the recession started to bite hard, and work was becoming increasingly tight.

Recession

The firm I worked for was closing down, so I was made redundant, so now I'm out of work, what am I supposed to do now. Two weeks later I received a phone call from Paul, we had a quick chat about how good our holiday was, but that wasn't the main reason he phoned. He said that he too had been made redundant from his firm, and was wondering if I could have a word with my boss, to see if he had any work for him. I told Paul that I was in the same boat as him, after a brief discussion we decided to look for work together.

So off we went, travelling around looking for work. After a couple of weeks with no luck, an offer came up, this was re-tiling old roofs on a big estate. This proved to be very hard, as we had to work on two story buildings without any scaffold. Although this was hard and pretty dangerous, we were earning really good money. After around three or four weeks I had enough, not just with that job, but with work in general. I then had a brilliant idea, why not buy a couple of jet-skis, and hire them out in Spain. But how am I supposed to pay for this, I didn't have that sort of money, so the answer to that was easy, I will get a loan.

But how am I supposed to pay for this, I didn't have that sort of money, so the answer to that was easy, I will get a loan. All my family, including May, was against the idea, saying that I haven't thought this through, but I was having none of it. I'm thinking, what is the matter with everyone, why can't they see that this is the best idea that I've ever had. I found out what jet-skis I wanted, I didn't want any old thing, I wanted the top of the range, and trailer to go with it. I don't know how I did it, but I managed to get a £20,000 unsecured loan.

So now I've got the cash it's off to buy the jet-skis, and a double trailer, but I didn't stop there, I also bought two banana boats for £1,000, and ten life jackets to boot. I sold my car to buy an old land-rover, so now I'm all set. Although May was against the idea, she wanted to come with me. One of my friends (Phil) that came on holiday to Lloret wanted to come with us, as he wanted to find work out there.

So we were all set for this venture to Lloret de mar. I had a fair amount of cash left over from the loan, so had enough to tide us over. On the day we loaded up the land-rover, we hooked up the trailer and said our goodbyes, then we were off, into the unknown on a 920-mile drive. I was absolutely buzzing with excitement, my adrenaline was flowing, and I felt like I was on top of the world.

The land-rover was built in 1969, and only went 60mph, either going up a steep hill, or down. The only time I stopped was for petrol and to grab a sandwich, you could say I was on a mission. We finally arrived in Lloret around 3pm, after 18 hours on the road. We stopped at a bar for a much-welcomed bottle of beer, and a bite to eat. We got chatting to the bar owner, who was English, (most of the bar owners there were English) and he said he had a lockup garage that we could rent. That was great, at least I had somewhere safe to keep the skis, now we had to sort out our accommodation.

Phil found a cheap room somewhere, as did May and I, but ours was above a nightclub, we only lasted a night there, as the noise was just too much, we then shared an apartment with another English guy that owned a bar. His name was Bob, or was known as good-on-ya Bob, reason being, that was his way of saying thank you. He was a bit of a character, and did like to powder his nose (if you get my meaning) before he opened his bar. May ended up working for him, while I was trying to get the skis up and running. It took us a couple of days of doing a bit of salesmanship and word of mouth, that we had a group of four-holiday makers wanting to hire the skis.

I knew I had to be careful not to take money on the beach, although I had insurance, I didn't have a permit. So we were paid up front in a bar, I charged £15 for 30 minutes, which was the going rate back in England. £60 for an hour, that was a lot of money back in the late 80s, we then made our way to the beach.

All went well until we were just about finished. The local police came on to the beach and asked who owned the skis, I said that I was the owner, what's the problem. They asked me if I was hiring them, in which I replied no, we were a group of friends. They didn't believe me, and said if I didn't remove them from the water, they will impound them. If they would have done that, it would have probably taken months to get them back. Plus I didn't want to upset them, I knew what the Spanish police were like, they would hit you with their batons first, then ask you questions after.

Not a good start, but it was early days. After a week or two of ducking and diving, and trying to avoid the police, we were introduced to a guy named Harvey. This guy owned a nightclub, plus he ran 18 to 30 club beach parties. He wanted a chat about a business proposal regarding the skis, and invited us to meet with him in his nightclub. We arranged a meeting at 7pm before the club opened, this was the next resort about seven miles away.

May and I drove down and arrived 10 minutes early, and was met at the entrance by a rather large doorman. He said in a gruff voice that the club was not open yet, but kindly opened the door when I said we had a meeting with Harvey. This place looked very seedy indeed, there were two more doormen on the inside, which gave us a bit of a menacing stare, and Harvey standing at the bar talking to the barmaid. He then spotted us and come over, and with a big smile on his face he said, "it's nice to see you, order whatever you want from the barmaid, take a seat, and I will be with you shortly".

We did as he said, and sat down at a table. A few minutes later Harvey joined us and proceeded to the business proposal. He asked us if we would be interested in hiring the skis at his beach parties, which would be two to three times a week. We said that we would be interested, and to tell us more. He said whatever we made, he wanted a 30% cut. I thought we might as well give it a go, as we could make quite a bit at one of these parties, so I said yes, we will give it a go. Harvey said to give him a few days and he will be in touch, so we finished our drinks, then left.

The next day I told Phil what was going on, in which he replied that he will ask around as well. A day later I heard from Harvey, he asked me if we would meet him at 11am at the beach next to his nightclub, and to bring the skis with me, I said "yes we will see you at 11". All three of us arrived on the beach at 10:50am, Phil needed the toilet so off he went. As May and I walked towards the beach bar, I could see Harvey with a couple of his heavies standing at the bar.

As we approached them, Harvey spotted us and didn't look happy, he then said, "Who the fuck is Phil?" I said he is a friend of mine, why what's he done, Harvey then said, he has been told that someone named Phil has been knocking on the doors of the 18to 30s club reps, and asking them if they wanted to do a deal with the jet-skis. He then said that he didn't appreciate someone asking the reps this, as he hasn't spoken to them about it yet.

Just as he said this Phil walked over and stood beside us. Harvey asked him who he was, before I could say anything Phil introduced himself. Harvey then said in a stern voice, "Oh so your Phil, good job you are a friend of Clive because if you weren't, YOU WOULD HAVE HAD A BASEBALL BAT WRAPPED AROUND YOUR FUCKING HEAD". By this time, Harvey's henchmen stood either side of Phil, I felt sorry for him as he went white as a sheet, and said, sorry he didn't realise. I also apologised and said this was my fault, as I asked Phil to ask around.

Harvey then calmed down and said, this was an inconvenience but not to worry, but this has lost a day of hiring the skis. He said that he will be in touch with another date for a beach party. So we left, and we couldn't get away from there quick enough. I never did hear from Harvey again, and to tell the truth, I was glad, I think he was into some pretty dodgy stuff. So it was back to ducking and diving with the skis, and I started to feel a bit low at this point. Then I was introduced to a Spanish guy who rented small speed boats and pedalos. We did a deal, 60/40 in my favour of what the skis earn. Although I had to travel 20 miles to where he was based, it was the only option I had.

On the first day, I drove up with the skis, which took about an hour. We had a chat on how this was going to work, and it was decided that I would deal with all the English speaking tourists, and him and his workers would deal with everyone else. The hours of work were 11am to 5:30pm, which I thought was great, only six and a half hour day. The first day went great, the skis were out for four hours, £240 so my cut was £144, not bad for sitting on the beach for 6.5 hours. I thought that this was going to be easy, how wrong I was.

After a couple of days, I was coming home shattered, this was actually hard work. What with an hour drive there, being in the sun for 6.5 hours, then an hour drive home, plus this is seven days a week. I would arrive home around 6:30 then have a three hour sleep, then have a shower and go and meet May in the new bar she worked in. This bar was under new ownership by a Spanish couple, (Seb

& Isabel), and the bar was called el galleon, Jon & Val's bar. May virtually ran the bar, and I used to help change the barrels. The tourists (mainly Dutch) used to think that we were Jon & Val, so we started to go along with it. May said to me, if I wasn't in the bar, people used to say "where's Jon?" I think I started to believe that I was actually Jon.

May finished work around 3am, and Seb would take us all for something to eat. I was up at 9am, have some breakfast before my journey into work. One particular day when I was at work, I was told that we needed to let the Guardia civil on the skis free of charge, when I asked why he said they will leave us alone. It was then I realised that he didn't have a permit to hire the skis.

One thing I didn't want to do was upset the Guardia civil, they were a lot worse than the police.

The next day one of the Guardia civil turned up with his young son, and wanted a ride on one of the skis. He was in uniform, and had to go and change. When he came back, I tried my hardest not to laugh. He had the skimpiest pair of yellow budgie smugglers on I have ever seen. All was going well for a month or so, then it all came crashing down around me. Someone had a bad accident on a jet-ski further up the coast, which hospitalised a Spanish windsurfer.

After that, the authorities banned all hiring of jet- skis along the coast, "shit", what am I supposed to do now. I have come all this way to hire jet- skis, I'm not going to do anything else. I tried every trick in the book to hire them out, but it was no good, the police were patrolling on every beach I took them to. I was getting very frustrated, and started to feel a bit depressed. A couple of very dodgy offers came my way, from some very dodgy characters.

First one was from two smartly dressed English guys in suits. They told me that they were in the export trade, and one of their lorries had broken down a few miles down the coast. The cargo was crates of Fosters lager, and it needed to be shifted. They said that if I could ask around in the bars if they were interested in buying some, they would pay me a good commission. I thought there was no harm in asking, so I did.

Some bar owners said they might be interested, but they wanted a sample first, which is fair enough, you're not going to buy something without sampling it first. I told the guys that I needed to take some samples to the bars, but they said it would take them a couple of days to be able to do this. They told me once they have the samples, they would be in touch, I never saw them again.

The next offer was to drive a lorry full of fish over the Spanish border, for a payment of £20,000. I thought this sounds great, but something worried me, and it wasn't the fish, it was what was in them that concerned me. So I said thanks, but no thanks. I knew I wasn't going to hire the skis, and then the dawn of realisation started to sink in. Money had almost run-out when I said to May I think it's best if we go home.

We didn't want to do this, but what else could we do, I come here to hire jet-skis, nothing else and so we decided to go home. Phil stayed out there working in a bar, and we only had enough money for petrol and ferry crossing. The journey home was not going to be a pleasant one. It must have been late evening when we were driving on a dark road, somewhere near Paris. We heard a loud pop, and my heart sank. I was praying it wasn't one of the trailer wheels, as I already used the spare on a previous puncture. These wheels were solid and unrepairable, I couldn't find anywhere that sold that size.

We pulled over, and I grabbed my torch as there were no lights on this road. Yep brilliant, it was the trailer wheel, we are in the middle of nowhere, no money, very hungry and thirsty, now this. So I said to May, I'm going to have to find an SOS phone to get help. We had a few bottles of warm beer in the back of the land- rover, but no bottle opener, so I smashed the tops off two, so we could at least wet our lips. Then we started to walk down this pitch black road, with nothing but thick dense trees either side of us.

We kept hearing twigs snapping in amongst the trees, which was quite spooky, then noticed that we were walking a little bit quicker than before. We must have walked close to a mile, but seemed a lot longer, before we come across a SOS phone. I picked up the receiver and said "parlez vous English". It took them a while, but someone did speak a little English, I told them what had happened, and they said someone will come out and help.

We then walked back to our car and waited. It must have been an hour later, when a truck pulled up and this guy stepped out. All I can say is, he looked like a character from the film, "the hills have eyes". He spoke very little English, but I could just understand what he said. He could not repair or replace the wheel, I would have to leave the skis at his garage, and go back home to buy a spare. I did not like the idea of this, but he assured me they would be safe, plus I had no option. I explained to him I had no money to pay him, to which he replied, I could pay him on my return. I agreed to leave them with him, so he hooked up my trailer and we took them to his garage, then dropped us back to where we were parked, we then headed for Calais.

When we finally made it to Calais, we were both very hungry and thirsty. We boarded the ferry and got seated in the bar area. There was a family sitting opposite us, and they had a young boy eating sausage and chips. We could smell the food, which was making us feel hungrier. Then the boy dropped the sausage and it rolled under his seat, I swear if that family had got up and left, we would have shared that sausage between us.

We finally made it onto British soil, and it seemed very strange driving on the left-hand side of the road again. Our first port of call was my sisters, they were very pleased to see us, but we couldn't speak properly until we raided her food cupboard. I returned to pick the skis up a week later. I paid £1,000 for those banana boats, and didn't use them once. May and I stayed with my mum for a while, as May's mum had moved to Scotland.

The recession had really hit the building trade, as there wasn't much work anywhere. All I could get was odd days here and there, plus May was also struggling to find work as a legal secretary. Things were not working out living with my mum, so May went to live with her mum in Scotland. After a month of frequently speaking to May on the phone, I decided to visit her in Scotland. That visit turned into a two-month stay, but I had to come back to sort out the jet-skis. They were locked up on my mum's front lawn, but one-night thieves tried to steal them. They cut the chain that secured the trailer and managed to drag them into the road where they tried to hook them up to their vehicle.

But luckily I had a lock on the trailer so they couldn't connect it to their tow bar.

Next morning Dick found the trailer and skis lying on the road. When I arrived back home, I managed to find a cheap lockup to rent, to store the skis. After being home for a few weeks, May phoned me with some news, "SHE WAS PREGNANT". I would like to say I was happy, but at the time I thought, 'May's in Scotland, I have no work, no money, nowhere for us to live, and now I'm going to be a dad, what else is going to happen'. So now I'm frantically searching to find us somewhere to live.

I managed to find a one bedroom flat in Southend, it was furnished, and clean, at least now, we could be together. May travelled down by train a week later, and I met her at the train station.

Although the flat was furnished, there wasn't a great deal of kitchenware. One day May wanted boiled eggs and soldiers, but we didn't have any egg cups. Then I had a great idea, I cooked the eggs and served them on two empty milk bottles. We weren't there long when another place came up in Basildon.

This was a bedsit, but the location was better than the last place. I was still struggling to find work, this recession had a tight grip, and I was lucky if I worked one day a week. Then I had a great idea, I'm going to make concrete garden ornaments. So I found out and bought what materials I needed and started to make a mould. Of all places to make it, I chose the kitchen, on a warm summer evening.

The smell of the fibreglass and resin was very strong, even with the kitchen window wide open, I had to keep having a break to get some fresh air. I had the fibreglass stuck everywhere, it was stuck to my hands, thus it was stuck to the door handles. About 30 minutes after I started, there was a loud knock at the door. May was in the bath, so she couldn't answer the door.

So I fumbled with front door handle, trying not to get too much fibreglass on it. Standing in front of me was a tall policeman, who said there had been a complaint about a strange smell coming from my kitchen, he then said that he needed to come in and investigate. So when he came in and I explained what the smell was, we both had a chuckle, and he said, it wasn't a very good idea to do this in a confined space like my kitchen, I agreed with him and said I probably won't make any more in there after this one, so the copper went on his merry way, and the mould turned out alright in the end.

Becoming a dad

On 11/12/1991 my son (Grant) was born, WOW, I'm a dad. Although we couldn't afford it, the day he was born, I rushed out to buy him the most expensive silk cot bedding I could find. A few weeks had passed, then I had another brilliant idea. I will open up a fruit and veg shop. So I began to look for shops to rent, it took a while but found a place in Shoeburyness, which is near Southend. This shop used to be a hairdresser's salon, but it would soon be converted to what I wanted it for.

So I set about the place with my trusted hammer and saw. I was quite pleased with the way the shop was looking, I had loads of shelves with green Astroturf type carpet in them. I did go a bit mad with the fixings, I smashed a load of nails through the bottom of the frame into the nice Lino flooring "oops", I didn't think the owners were going to be very pleased with me, "oh well", it looked good to me.

Finally, all done, I had got my tilt and scales, now all I had to do was fill it with fruits and veggies. So off I went to my local wholesalers, I think I must have been slightly overloaded, my axels were on the floor, and my tyres were flat, I think I only had a box of bananas in the boot. Oh I meant to say, I only had a Fiat 127, and to think about it now I bet the people that worked at the wholesalers were laughing their heads off.

There were all these green grocers' big vans and trucks parked to load up, and there was me struggling to get a couple of boxes of bananas in my little fiat 127. Anyway, the shop didn't last that long as there was a big Asda's up the road that I think killed business. I used to sit there all day to sell a bunch of bananas and two onions, I was throwing more produce away than I was selling, it was quite a while before I realised why I wasn't selling anything until I went into Asda's. For instance I found that they were selling their iceberg lettuces cheaper than I pay for them wholesale, so I used to shop at Asda's for certain items. I was out of there after a couple of months.

Grant was 18 months old when we were offered a three bedroom house, in which we said yes to the offer straight away. We couldn't believe our luck when we went to view the property, this place was brand new. We had no furniture, appliances, or money to buy these things. May's uncle kindly offered to give us a loan for a cooker, so at least we could cook. We were sitting on deckchairs for quite a while before we could afford to buy some second hand furniture. I was working whenever I could, but there still wasn't a great deal of work about. 15/02/1994 is when my daughter (Kayleigh) was born, yet another proud moment.

It was at this time when Dick sadly passed away. This was very sudden, and a shock for everyone. My mum was really struggling at the time, as she had broken her arm and had it in plaster. I think she was feeling very vulnerable, as she could not do simple things like opening a tin. I used to phone her every day to see how she was, and she would say that she was just lying on the bed. I would say to her, that I will come over and pick her up to bring her to my house. She was feeling very lonely, and I knew that she didn't want to be on her own. She was with us more than she was at home at that time.

One good thing is that Dick and I got on quite well just before he passed. He even used to help me out in the fruit & veg shop on some occasions. He used to enjoy coming to the shop, I think it kept him busy, as he didn't have anything else to do at that time. It took a long time for my mum to get used to being on her own. I used to feel so bad when I had to leave her and come home.

A few years had passed, and the roofing industry was at an all-time low. I needed to work, so I took a job offer as a hod carrier. I don't know if any non-British readers would know what a hod carrier is. In layman terms it's a bricklayer's labourer and the hood is a box with a staff that you carry on your shoulder. I don't know what was manually harder, roofing, or hod-carrying. After a few months, I started to get the hang of the job, so much so the foreman made me coddy-hoddy, which is head hod carrier. I was really working hard, and that reflected in my wages.

I was earning the same as a bricklayer, but working like two hoddies on some days. Looking after four bricklayers was not an easy task and I would literally be running with a hod for most of the day. Although it was a tough day at work, I started running again. I was arriving home from work, having my dinner, then a couple of hours later, I would be on a 10-mile run. I had so much energy, that I had to burn it off somehow.

This went on for quite a while, until one day at work, in the afternoon I felt really sick and very shaky and had to sit down for a while. When I felt slightly better, I had a sudden craving for an isotonic drink, so I stopped work and walked to a local store to buy one. Soon as I finished the drink I felt a lot better, then thought to myself, it must have been my blood sugar level had dropped.

I felt fine for the rest of the day and carried on working as normal. A few days had passed and I was becoming increasingly irritable, this was at work and at home. I started to struggle at work, with everyday tasks that I would normally do with ease. I was feeling drained of energy, and becoming a bit aggressive towards my co-workers.

Now I felt really depressed, I would wake up in the morning, get ready for work, and break down in tears. I thought that I can't do this anymore, I don't want to go to work. I started to lose weight, I only recognised this when I was in the bath, as it hurt the bones in my buttocks. This was winter, and it was (-3) degrees outside, I went out to put a refuse bin in the garage, and I was wearing just a pair of shorts. When I came back into the house, I was literally dripping with sweat.

One day at work I went to lift a concrete block, and I just couldn't pick it up, I thought what is the matter with me, I used to carry 3 of these at a time all day long, then I had to go home. This went on for a couple of weeks, and my boss said that I should go to the doctor, he said that I must be ill because I just can't do the job that I previously was so good at. At this point I think I said to him in so many words, that he was talking out of his arse, then I went home.

I started to get heart palpitations, this was especially worse at night, when I was in bed, I could hear and feel my heart beating in my ear drums. May was so worried about me and made me an appointment to see the doctor. As soon as the doctor listened to my heart beat, I was put on beta blockers. Then my blood test results revealed that I had an overactive thyroid, the doctor told me that it was so bad, that it was off the scale. I was then put on medication, and had to have regular blood tests. I was off work for a while, but I knew that I couldn't go back to being a hod carrier again.

Another job offer came up through a friend, this was in a factory environment, and the job was a machine operator. This involved working a mailing machine, cutting, folding, and inserting bank statements into envelopes. This was working a night shift, from Sunday to Thursday. This was something completely different to what I was used to, but there was full training on how to run the machines. The first couple of nights was awful, I hated it and said to May that I was not cut out for this sort of thing, she said to give it a chance and see how it goes. I could not get my head around the training, my mind would just go blank, I just couldn't remember what I had learnt.

My training period was over, and I thought that the trainer was going to say, I was not cut out for this role. But instead I was let loose on the machines, it took me a few days to get the hang of them, but they weren't too bad after all. Before long I was up for an award for producing the most bank statements in a shift.

May got friendly with a lady in our street, and they would go to the bingo hall together. One particular night they both decided to go to a clairvoyance evening. I stayed at home to look after the kids, and it was getting quite late, so I went to bed. I was only there for about ten minutes when May came home. She came into the bedroom to see if I was still awake, and I asked her how her evening was.

Now, what I'm about to write still freaks me out 17 years later. When I asked her about her evening she said, the clairvoyant picked her out from a room full of people and said "Do the names Anne or Queenie mean anything to her?", May said "no", then the clairvoyant said, "there is a man here, his said his name is Charlie, and he said he has been trying to contact the boy for a very long time, Charlie wants to say that he is at peace with his foot."

As soon as May said that to me, I sat bolt upright in bed and I could feel the hairs on the back of my neck lifting off my skin, WHAT THE FUCK. How did, and how could this woman know about this, FOR FUCK SAKE, even May didn't know about my dad's foot. And as for Anne and Queenie, that was my dad's sister's names. This is another thing that I cannot explain, and I can't get my head around it to this day. May bought a tape recording of this conversation, which I still have in the attic somewhere.

The year is 1999, and May and I wanted to try for another baby. As I had a thyroid problem, and I was on medication, we went to ask the doctor if this would be ok, and the doctor said it wouldn't be a problem. So on 25/02/2000 our 2nd son (Mason) was born, and he did not want to hang around, May was in labour for 20 minutes. Mason had some funny little ways when he was a toddler. We had to leave the bin lid open, so his sweet wrappers could see out. He wouldn't put rubbish in a bin outside, it had to be put in our bin at home.

We couldn't throw any of his old clothes or shoes away, we had to keep them in a spare drawer.

On his first day at nursery, he managed to walk out and follow May up the road. She didn't even know he was behind her, until someone said to her, "is that your little boy following you". Walking out of school on his first day, all sounds very familiar to me, maybe he is a chip off the old block.

When Mason was in infant school, May had to tell him that she would sit outside the school, and wait for him all day until he finished, that was the only way we could get him to go. When his class went for an induction day at the juniors, the teacher gave all the class some paper to draw a picture. But Mason point blank refused to do it, he said "that was boring, so I'm not doing it". He did finally settle down in school.

RIP Mum

This was a very dark time for me when I lost my mum. I was due to visit mum in the evening, but I came home from work early so I decided to go see her around 1pm. When I arrived and knocked on the front door, she didn't answer. My mum kept a spare door key hidden under a flower pot for emergencies, so I used that to gain entry. As I walked through to the hallway, I found mum lying on the floor, she was between the kitchen and hallway.

I feared the worst as she was white as a sheet, I fell to my knees beside her and screamed, "MUM, MUM". She tried to speak, but she was just mumbling, I breathed a sigh of relief to hear her voice. I immediately phoned for an ambulance, and she was rushed to the hospital. I don't know how long she had been lying there for, but it must have been for hours. She was still in her dressing gown, she normally got dressed around 8am.

Julie went with her in the ambulance, and I followed in my car. When we arrived at the hospital things took a turn for the worst. Mum had a heart attack while she was being assessed, and the doctors had to revive her. They said at home she probably had a stroke, but she also had hypothermia, where she was lying on the floor for so long. She was also badly bruised down one side, where she fell. She was in the hospital for almost six weeks, where she briefly made some improvements. But then she wasn't responding to any treatment, and she kept asking that she wanted to go home.

The doctors wanted to speak to Julie and I, and said that mum would be better off at home, as they couldn't do anymore to help her. In other words my mum wanted to spend her final days in the comfort of her own home, so we arranged for her to come home. She had to have oxygen bottles delivered, and a special inflatable mattress. The first night Julie was going to stay with her, so I went home to sort a few things out. I was only home for 30 minutes when Julie phoned me and said mum was asking for me, so I went straight back to see her.

When I arrived there mum said that she was sorry to ask for me, and she was just being silly. I told her that she wasn't being silly and that I will stay with her. On the second day mum had to have morphine administrated through a syringe drive. That knocked her completely out, she just slept all the time after that.

Julie and I took turns to go home for a quick shower, which only took about an hour. The nurses that used to come in left us a booklet, this was information on loved ones final days and hours. Julie had gone home and I was sitting by mum's bedside and I began to read the book. It said that although your loved one seemed to be sleeping, they do know that you are there. It said to talk to the person, as they will be able to hear you, even though they can't answer.

So I sat there talking to mum and holding her hand, and I knew she could hear me, as she would give a slight smile when I spoke. Julie returned and came into the bedroom, I said to her that mum had been smiling, so Julie sat talking to her. I said to Julie that I'm going home for a shower, I'll be about an hour. In fact, it was 50 minutes when I returned, and as I opened the front door I could hear Julie crying. I then knew that my mum had passed and rushed into the bedroom. My mum never liked to sleep lying flat down and always slept with her head propped up with two or three pillows.

There she was propped up in bed with a slight smile on her face, with her eyebrows slightly raised. I let out a cry, and said, "NOOOOO, MUMMY". I don't know why I said that, as I never called her mummy, even when I was a little boy. Julie left me with mum for a while, and I sat holding her hand. I said to her, why did you leave me when I wasn't here, I was only gone for 50 minutes. I sat there for ages holding her hand, to the point my mum was getting cold.

So I said to her that I will keep her warm, and pulled the covers over her arms. But no matter how hard I tried to keep my lovely mum warm, it was no use, she was still getting cold. I had to leave her, but

I didn't want to then the doctor came and needed to examine her. I had to prize my mum's hand off mine, as I had wrapped her fingers around my hand and I didn't want to let her go.

As I'm writing this I've had to stop and wipe the tears from my screen, as it's like it was just yesterday. If my mum did have a guiding spirit like she was told, and had a premonition like my nan, I don't think she would have realised, as she was too drugged up with morphine on the final two days of her life. The death of my dear mum really affected me, and I felt deeply depressed, I just felt numb, physically and mentally.

A chip off the old block

My boys loved to play football, but also found that they had a natural talent in running. Kayleigh is the academical one, and not into sport, but I need to mention her as she will think I have left her out, she makes up for it with her kind nature. Grant started when he was 15, and joined our local athletic club. Mason started when he was 9, as he used to come to watch Grant and wanted to join in. They are distance runners just like I was, and are particularly good at cross country.

They both worked hard and got to county level, and won quite a few county championship titles between them. I remember Grant's first cross country race for his club, we arrived at the venue, and I couldn't find his club tent. I started to panic as it was getting close to his race time, then I spotted it. We were met by the team manager, who introduced himself as Bill, He gave Grant his race numbers and wished him luck. Grant had a good race and finished in the top 10 out of around 60 runners, that was a decent performance for his first race. Grant carried on improving to become a county standard athlete, and represented the county of Essex in some major championship meetings.

Mason also followed in his brother's footsteps and earned his county vest. He has won gold in some county championship meetings. A few years had passed and they both still are working hard and reaping the fruits of their efforts. We see Bill quite a lot for a few years at all the meetings, and at the club. I was on Facebook one day and Bill popped up on there, so I sent him a friend request. He already had Grant and Mason as friends on there, so I thought I might as well send him a request. Bill accepted me so I thought I would be nosy and take a look at his photos. He had quite a lot of old photos of when he was a runner many years ago.

Then I looked at this one photo in particular, as Bill was wearing a tee shirt that said British American Marathon, with a logo of two hands shaking, one with a Union Jack on it, and the other with the Stars and Stripes. I had the very same tee shirt that was given to me after the Canvey Marathon many years ago. Then I looked closely at Bill's face in the photo, I thought could it be? No surely not, but it did look like the guy that got me to the finish line that day 32 years ago.

I sent Bill a Facebook message to ask him if he did that race on Canvey. He then replied yes he did, so I asked him if he can remember running the whole race with a skinny 16-year-old. He then replied, yes he can remember running with a young lad. So I replied back to him saying, that skinny 16-year-old was me, and I have photos of the two of us. He couldn't believe it when I sent the photos to him, all that time I knew Bill, I had no idea that he was, "the guy", as I called him back then. It's a small world.

Left: Mason on his way to winning the county champs u15 3000m and setting the fastest UK time of the season. Right: Grant on the podium with his trophy, for winning the county champs senior 5000m final. One proud dad.

With my boys doing well, and my background in running, I started to think about becoming a coach. Although I hated anything to do with courses or of a classroom nature, I booked a two-day assistant coach course. I couldn't book a level two coaching course until I completed the level 1 first. I wanted to become a top athletics coach, I was pretty much deluded at the time. I thought, how hard can this be, I know what training is needed to progress from one level of fitness to the next.

I have been around coaches at the club for a number of years, where I picked up on a lot of their training techniques. So I completed the course and got my assistant coach licence through the post. Brilliant, now I've got my licence I can start coaching on my own. I was doubting Mason's coach, and thinking that I could do a better job. I first asked Mason if he was happy with his training, and he replied that he wasn't. So I took him out of the group and started coaching him myself. It was going well for a couple of months, but he needed to train with others, rather than on his own.

So I asked Grant's coach if Mason could join his group, in which he said, yes that would be fine. Mason fitted in well in this group, plus there was a lot more structure to their training plan. I started to spend all day doing online researching in coaching, writing out training plans, and buying e-books. I set up a website offering online coaching, I made this priority over everything else.

I started to coach a group of young athletes at the club, as well as helping out other coaches. None of the training plans I wrote out was ever finished, in my eyes they would get boring, so I would start a new one. All this didn't last long, as it all just got too boring so I gave it all up. I didn't even want to go to the club anymore where I used to enjoy watching my boys train for around seven years previously.

Train crash

What is all this ice bucket challenge I keep hearing about? I kept seeing these people throwing buckets of water filled with ice over their heads. At first, I thought this was a bit silly really, until one day I decided to do it myself. But I didn't just want to throw a bucket of water over my head, I had to go one better. I had a 500 litre water butt in my shed that I borrowed from a building site a few years ago, I'm going to fill that with water, chuck a few bags of ice in, then put my ladder up the back of my house, climb up as high as I dare, and dive straight in, now that's what I call an ice bucket challenge.

May tried to talk me out of it, saying I must be mad, and it's too dangerous, but I thought it would be a good challenge, as I was going to get Grant to film it, then post it on Facebook. So I set the ladder up, went to the shed to retrieve the water butt and hose, then I thought that I would do a dummy run. I climbed up to just above the ground floor window, and thought this looks quite high, but let's go higher, so up I went level with the bedroom window, yep this is high enough. I then connected the hose and turned the water on low. Then I decided to quickly go to the store to buy a few bags of ice.

When I got back the garden was like a swimming pool and the water butt was empty. When I looked closely at the bottom of the butt, I noticed a big crack in it. I tried to seal the crack with gaffer tape, but it was no good, the water was still pouring out. So that was the end of that idea, and I was pretty disappointed. I did end up doing the challenge, but had to use a couple of boring buckets.

A few months had passed, and I was looking through the local newspaper. There was a whole page advertising this scare attraction, which was only a couple of miles away from where I live. My daughter Kayleigh loves things like this, so I thought I would look on their website. Well, this looked pretty good, there were about six different themed mazes that you walk through with live actors that jumped out at you. I thought I must tell Kayleigh about this.

Then at the bottom of the page it said "Why not become a scare actor?" What a brilliant idea, I will become a scare actor, so I sent them an email. The next day I got a reply, they invited me to a sort of audition, which I attended. This was absolutely hilarious, there must have been around 20 of us sitting around in a circle, where for about 15 minutes the trainer explained what it takes to become a scare actor. Then we had to chase one another around this hall, trying to scare them. I'm actually pissing myself with laughter while writing this.

We then had to demonstrate, what we thought, it would be like trapped in a coffin. Now we are all lying on the floor shouting and screaming, "LET ME OUT, LET ME OUT". Picture this, there are all these 'would be' scare actors in their 20s, and me 49 years old rolling around on the floor, bloody hilarious. Anyway the audition took around three hours, then we were told the ones that are successful would be contacted.

Thought "well that was that", I probably won't hear no more from them. Guess what, around a week later I received an email and it said, "Congratulations you were successful in becoming a scare actor". My first thought was, 'oh fuck what have I let myself in for'. Anyway the night before the attraction opened, I had to go down to talk about what character I would be, plus pick up my costume. So it was decided, I would be in a maze called "THE WORK CHOP", and my character was a mad butcher, I thought this is quite fitting really. There wasn't a lot in the costume bag, I had a pair of black trousers, a butcher's white coat, and an apron. I was then told that I needed to supply my own props, e.g. toy knife or meat cleaver.

The only prop I could find at short notice was a silly little toy knife. I arrived an hour before the grand opening, as I needed that time for the makeup artists to work their magic on me, I thought, "well", I don't need a lot done in that department. There were loads of actors getting their makeup done, and I was introduced to another butcher that was going be in the maze with me.

My partner in crime was Callum, he was an experienced scare actor that had been the butcher for a couple of years. I thought great, there's me with my little toy knife, and there's Callum with all his own custom made costume, with a massive meat cleaver. Oh, by the way, we were told under no circumstances must we bring in real props.

Right here I am, makeup all done, (I looked like a blood smothered corpse), my costume was covered in fake blood, and I'm ready to go. There were four of us, two butchers, one receptionist, and some weird looking character, not sure what he was really. We were then led by the manager to our maze. It was spooky in this maze, it had this weird loud music playing, and it had strobe lighting that flicked on and off. Callum and I decided that he would work at the front of the maze, and I would be inside, this suited me as I had the whole run of the place.

The layout of the maze was, the people would come through a reception area, where there were loads of fake human body parts hanging up and down a long hallway, it also had a bath filled with fake blood and bits of body parts. Then they had to go into this room which was like a mini maze with body parts hanging up, plus it was hard to find the exit. Also in this room were places that you could hide in, I thought this would be a good place to play peek-a-boo.

It was hard to see in this maze, when the strobe lighting flickered, it gave the effect off, "now you see me, now you don't. Also in this maze there was plenty of concealed doorways, so one minute you could be in one place, then all of a sudden appear somewhere else.

So we were all setup, Callum with his big meat cleaver at the entrance and me with my pathetic little knife in this room, now we had about five minutes before they opened, and our maze was the first one the people would enter. I was quite nervous at this point, my adrenaline was pumping and I had butterflies in my stomach, then the first group came in.

The receptionist would speak to the people quite loud, that was to let me know inside that they were coming. I could hear them screaming as the 4th guy on our team was running in and out of the doorways jumping out at them. Then they entered my room, they couldn't see me as I was standing behind a partition. I could hear these girls saying they didn't like it, they sounded really scared, which is what we wanted to achieve.

I then jumped out like a deranged maniac waving my scary looking knife, and growled at the top of my voice "aaaaaaarrrrrrr". There was a group of girls and they all screamed at the top of their voices, they started running around in this room but couldn't find the exit. This was so funny as they ended up running out the way they come in, they then had to come back in the room, so I jumped out at them again, I think they were more scared the second time. They finally found the way out, with a bit of help from me.

Then a second group came in, this was a group of men as I could hear them saying "this isn't very scary in here". They entered my room where I was behind the partition, I let them walk past me, where I could see them, but they didn't spot me. I was trying not to laugh as it looked quite comical, they had limited vision so they were walking in a crouched position.

They weren't so vocal now, it was silent, so I thought I would target the guy at the back. Bearing in mind these guys were quite big and beefy, I thought I better watch myself here as I didn't want to end up on my arse. I did the same thing I had done with the girls, I've never seen anything so funny in my life. These big guys all screamed worse than the girls, and the guy I targeted pleaded with me to leave him alone as he was so scared, that is the god's honest truth.

By this time I was really getting into character, plus the more people I scared the more manic I was getting. A couple of hours past, and a lot of people came and went, some were scared some not so scared. We finished around 11pm after a four hour shift, with a few quick breaks in between.

When I got home I still had all the makeup on, May looked at me and shook her head, perhaps she thought I didn't look a lot different. I had a shower and it took ages to get the makeup off. Then I sat downstairs and enjoyed a few bottles of beer. Then (this is how my head works) I started to think, I could make that maze ten times better than it is. I would put holes in the ceiling so I could drop right down in front of people.

I would have an actor on a table having his leg sawn off, fake one of course. Have a girl actor being dragged behind a partition, where she would be beheaded, there would be a fake head on the floor where I would come back out holding it up like some sort of trophy. I know all this sounds a bit gruesome, but this is a scare attraction at the end of the day.

When I woke up the next morning I couldn't speak. With all the shouting I did the night before, I had a sore throat. I was back in the maze that night, but I wanted a better knife to the one I had. I wanted something that looked real, I said to myself, I know I'll take a real one in. I know they said we weren't allowed them, but they won't know if I sneak one in will they. So I looked in the drawer and found a nice big kitchen knife, plus a knife sharpener.

It came to me what I was going to do. When people entered the maze and found themselves in the hallway, all they would see at the other end was me. I thought this will look good, what with the strobe lights flashing and the weird music playing, I'm going to stand there with a sinister grin on my face sharpening my knife, then I will disappear into the room, which should spook them I thought.

So that night I pulled up in the car park right next to the maze, which was handy for me to get the knife. I went in to get the makeup on, then a couple of minutes before we were due to start I went to get the knife. That worked out great, I managed to smuggle the bag which had the knife and sharpener in. So we were all in position waiting for our first victims to arrive.

I heard the call from the receptionist, I thought right here we go. The first group appeared at the other end of the hallway, this group was a mixture of men and women. One of them shouted out "Jesus there's a bloke down there with a knife, they all just stood there looking very uneasy as I sharpened my knife very loudly, I started cackling like a madman and said, FRESH MEAT, then beckoned them to walk towards me with my finger.

They just froze there, so as soon as the lights flashed off, I disappeared into the room. It seemed like ages until I heard them just outside the room. Then I see a head appear, but I know they can't see me as I'm behind the partition. Then a few more of the group appeared, then I think they were all in the room but they still couldn't see me.

Then I could see this guy who looked familiar, "fuck" I know him it's James who trains with my lads at the running club. Then I sprung out from behind the partition which in turn made the group jump and scream out. Bearing in mind no one can see properly, and I've got my face made up, I said in a sinister voice, "I hope you have been training hard JAMES". Well, I wish I could have taken a picture of his face, I could tell exactly what he was thinking, "HOW THE FUCK DOES THIS MAD

LOOKING BUTCHER, WIELDING A KNIFE KNOW MY NAME", that was priceless.

When I next saw James I did tell him that I was that mad butcher, which did take him a while to believe. I thought I'm getting good at this, I was running around in there like a madman and getting paid for it, although it was only £20 a night. I had 3 nights of being a mad butcher and thoroughly enjoyed it.

After being on a high as the butcher, things slowly started to deteriorate. I started to feel pretty low, and didn't want to do the things that I used to enjoy. I would take Mason to the club for his training session, and just sit in the car whereas before, I would enjoy watching him train. I didn't want to see anyone there because that would mean I would have to talk to them, and say how everything is alright when it wasn't, I needed to do something, but what?

One of my old friends from the Kings club days lived in Spain, and he seemed to have a much better way of living than me. Then I had a great idea, why don't we all move to Spain. I know now this was a crazy idea, but at that time this was the best idea that I had ever had. I discussed this with May, but she was dead against my plans. I could not understand why anyone would think that staying here, putting up with all this crap that was being thrown at us, was better than trying to better our lifestyle.

We were in a lot of debt, with bailiffs knocking on the door demanding money that we didn't have. Our landlord threatening to kick us out of our home, can't afford to buy food, the list goes on. I started to get deeply depressed with mixed emotions, one minute I was elated and excited with the thought of moving to Spain, next minute I felt angry, sad, and depressed, at the thought that no one else wanted to back me. I shut myself away from everyone, I didn't want to speak or see anyone, I would lay on my bed in floods of tears for no apparent reason. I thought that I can't carry on like this, if no one wants to move to Spain, then I will go on my own.

May and I had a joint bank account, so I decided to open a single account for when I was in Spain. Plus I will sell my car to give me some cash to get me started out there. One morning I left the house and went to the bank to open a new account. I sat with the clerk for ages filling in forms, only to get my application refused because we were up to our limit on the overdraft.

Great, what was I supposed to do now, if I got work out there and I could not pay any money into my account? Then I thought that I will cross that bridge when I came to it. As for selling my car, there was no time, I had to get away as soon as possible. Then it hit me, I thought my passport might have ran out, so I quickly searched the drawers until I found it, and to my relief there were still a few months left to the expiry date. May and I were constantly arguing, and the kids were constantly getting upset.

I asked them for their opinion on the move, but they didn't want to go, as they had their work and friends here. So I was on my own on this one, I was very upset that I was going to leave my family, but at the time I felt I had no choice. I only had enough cash for a one-way flight ticket, and a small amount of spending money, that might last for a week or so.

I couldn't stay in the house any longer, I had to get out before my head burst. So I packed a suitcase, said my goodbyes which was very upsetting, and headed for my sisters. This was around 8pm, and I decided that I would book the next available flight first thing in the morning. I must have been at my sister's for two hours, then I decided to call May and tell her that no matter what I do, I still love her and the kids deeply.

When we spoke, we were both getting very upset and May said the kids were very upset too. I then said that I would come back home to try and explain to them that I had to do this. When I arrived home I just broke down in tears, and said to May I think I need some help. The next day May made an emergency appointment for me to see the doctor. When I spoke to the doctor, he said I was suffering from severe depression. He also asked if I would agree to try antidepressants, in which I said yes, I would do anything to feel better.

So now I was on anti-depressants, I hoped these hurried up and started to work. I still felt at rock bottom for a while after I started the meds, but remembered the doctor did say they take some time to get into your system. I used to just sit in the chair all day long on my iPad looking at the screen, wondering what I could do. I ended up purchasing game apps on my iPad that I wasn't really interested in. I then would purchase coins and perks for the games, build them up to the best they could be, then I would get bored and delete them.

One game in particular was a war game that you play online components, where you would blow up their base, which was the name of the game. I would blow their base up no problem, but if they blew my base up, that was different. I would go mad, how dare they blow up my base, when it had taken me days and cost me money. I used to say to myself, I wish I could send them a shitty message. It sounds pathetic I know, but that was how I was at the time.

One day I decided to sell online, so I started thinking about what I could sell. Then it came to me, I will sell lady's lingerie, I know this sounds weird, but that was where my head was at that time. I didn't have any money to buy stock, so I found a supplier that I could buy from as I sold. I created a website and called it, Kayteez underwear, and I was Kay Tee, "only virtually".

I thought that a lot of people would probably be a bit embarrassed to walk into a shop to buy this sort of clothing, so this was a good thing to sell online. Plus people would probably prefer to deal with a good looking woman, so that is who I'll be, "Kay Tee, the virtual sexy lady that sells provocative lingerie". With my website, I also setup an eBay shop, so I was all set, and looking forward to opening day.

It turned out that I was getting more interest from the eBay shop, a couple of orders came in on the first day, and a few inquiries. Then I was getting inundated with some pretty weird requests, which I could only imagine were from dirty old men. I won't go into detail about what they were asking, I will leave that to your imagination. I started to really get into character when I was answering the requests, I actually became Kay, but without the clothing, I was getting a real buzz out of it.

I had one guy that was a transvestite that turned out to be my best customer. He was married with grownup children, but just liked to dress in women's lingerie. He came across as a nice guy, but he started to get a bit too familiar, also he asked me if I would be interested in sending him photos of me in my lingerie (if only he knew I was a fella). I thought this quite funny at the time and went along with it to begin.

I would find a photo of a sexy lady online (just a lady in underwear), then crop it so the face wasn't showing, and send it to him. At the end of the day, he was a good paying customer. I told him that he must understand that I cannot show my face, which he said he fully understood. Then he started to send me photos of himself in the lingerie that he had bought off me, which I most certainly did not want him to do. I told him not to send me anymore photos as I was married, and I would not want my husband to find them. He said that I could just delete them once I've seen them, but he said he won't send any if I didn't want him too.

It started to get too much when I would receive about 10 emails a day from this guy, and to top it all, he must have done some research online about me (Kay Tee). I didn't just setup a website, and an eBay shop, I also paid for some Google advertising, whereas I had to give my address, also I setup a Kayteez underwear Facebook account, which this guy was a friend on that page.

On this particular day, he sent me an email, asking me if Clive Webb was my husband. He stated that Clive Webb kept popping up on his Facebook page and he said that I was from the same place as this guy. "OH FUCK", what have I done, this guy thinks that I'm married to myself, he thinks that I'm my husband. May hasn't got a clue that I'm doing this, what if this guy shows up on my doorstep. I sent him an email back, and said that this has got to stop, as this is getting too close to home. He then replied that he was very sorry, he did not mean to upset me, he classed me as his friend, so that was the last thing he wanted to do. I told him that I was going to stop selling online, and I'm closing my website and eBay shop, he then stopped emailing me.

Shortly after this, May was diagnosed with emphysema, this is a serious lung disease, that we now know she had for a long time before the diagnosis. She had been misdiagnosed a few years earlier with asthma, but in fact was the early signs of this lung disease. This was devastating news for the both of us and for May in particular, because she always thought she had asthma. She was now registered disabled, and I am her full-time care giver.

This has affected us both mentally and physically. Some nights when I lay in bed next to May, and I hear her struggling to breathe, I have tears rolling down my cheeks because I feel so sorry for her, and I can't do anything to prevent this crippling disease. I started to get mixed emotions again, I'm feeling angry and sad, but high as a kite, all at the same time. Also, I'm getting really snappy with anyone that's around me, to the point that I needed to seek some help.

One evening it was so bad, I said to May that I was going to the hospital. May came with me to A&E, where I was seen by a psychiatrist. She asked me many questions, some I could answer, and some I couldn't. She told me that I needed to see the first response team at the mental health unit, she then said that she will send them a report, and I will hear from them very soon. We then left and went home.

I never had a chance to see the response team, as the very next night I flipped out. It must have been about midnight, and I was feeling very elated. May and I had a slight argument, it must have been something really small, as I can't even remember what it was about. But I had to get out of the house and had a walk to clear my head. On this walk, well I say walk, it was more of a power walk, I felt very high and elated. I wanted some excitement, my head was buzzing like I was on some sort of drug, I felt 30 years younger.

It was pitch black as the council turn the street lights off at this time of the night. I found myself walking towards the main town, which was about five miles from my house. Then it entered my head that I would try to get the police to chase me,

(I know this sounds stupid) I thought when I see a police car, I will jump out in front of it and goad them. About five minutes later I saw one, but I see it a bit too late, and it drove past, so I stopped and just stared at the driver as he went past, he just looked at me then drove off.

As I carried on speed walking, I see a figure through a car headlight in the distance walking towards me. As the figure got closer, I could see it was a guy with his hood up. He was on collision course with me, when we were about 20ft apart, I thought 'there's no way that I'm moving'. Then we crashed into each other, he must have been on his phone, as it flew out of his hand and landed on the path.

He was very startled as he didn't see me in my black clothes. He said sorry I didn't see you, then picked his phone up, I asked him if his phone was ok, and he replied "yes", then we were on our way. I was still buzzing at this point, and started to think that it might be a good idea to head to the hospital. I hadn't seen another police car for around 20 minutes, and had a chuckle to myself, as I thought 'where's a policeman when you need one'.

I actually ended up outside the police station, which is about two miles from the hospital, and I thought maybe they would kindly give me a lift the rest of the way, as all that speed walking had made my leg ache. I sat on the roadside opposite the station and had a cigarette, a couple of police cars came past me, they gave me a stare and carried on. I then walked over towards the entrance and tried the door.

It must have been 1am and the entrance to the station was locked, so I buzzed on the intercom. A woman answered and asked where I was, to which I replied, "I'm standing outside, where do you think I am!" she then said, "When you buzz the intercom, it goes through to head office". So I told her that I'm at the Basildon station, then she said someone will be with me shortly, I said thank you and stood there waiting. It must have only been less than a minute, and I got impatient, I thought that I would walk the rest of the way to the hospital.

Opposite the police station was a multi-storey car park, and I thought I've never actually walked up there before, I've only ever driven in my car. Now I found myself waking up the concrete stairs, I don't know why I was going up there at the time but I got to the very top, then I remembered that there was a tall metal safety fence around the car park. So I went one floor down and stood at the edge and looked over. I didn't realise how good the view was from up here, then I lit another cigarette, and leant over the edge to admire the view. I started to hear voices from down below.

So I looked down to see about eight policemen and women and they were looking up and down the road. At the time I thought this was quite comical, if only they were to look up, they would see me. I stood there for around a minute smoking my cigarette and watching these coppers walk up and down the road scratching their heads. So I thought I better give them a clue as to where I am, so I did a little whistle and eight heads all looked up at the same time.

This reminded me of a bird returning to its nest, and all the little chicks' heads pop up at the same time in search of food. Then a policewoman called up and said, "Are you alright mate?", then I replied "Yes", she said "What are you doing up there?" I said "Just admiring the view", she said,

"Can you step away from the edge?" I said "yes certainly, I wasn't going to jump, if that's what you're thinking".

Before I knew it I was surrounded by police, who searched me then walked me back down. When they asked me why I buzzed on the intercom, I said I needed to go to the hospital, and I was wondering if they would take me. They said yes they would, but first they need to contact my next of kin, and wanted all my details. I said that I don't want May to come to the hospital, as she has got her own problems, and she wasn't well enough to spend a second night down there. Then they said they were sending a squad car around to my house, which I wasn't too happy about.

About ten minutes later the police told me that they had spoken to May, and she is adamant that she was coming to the hospital, I wasn't happy about this, but they said they couldn't stop her, so off I went in the squad car to the hospital. When we arrived I was flanked by four coppers, and I felt like a criminal as I was getting stared at by people in the waiting room. I had to go into a separate room to fill in some forms, just before we went into the room the nurse said to the police, was it safe for her to go in with me. The police assured her that I was fine, but they came in as well, this made me feel like I was some sort of psychopath, but I could see her point, I suppose they get all sorts of people in there.

After I filled in the forms, I sat in the waiting room with a policeman sitting on both sides of me, and two standing in front. I said to them that I needed to go for a smoke, to which they replied that would be fine, but they need to accompany me. After my cigarette, we sat back down in the waiting room. It seemed like ages before May turned up with two more coppers and May said the police picked her up but on the way down they stopped a drunk driver and had to arrest them.

The doctor was asking me the same questions as the night before, to which I told her that I'd already answered those questions. I started to get agitated and restless, and my feet were tapping ten to the dozen. May tried to calm me down, but it was no good, I had to get out of there. I then stood up and said, I'm fed up with repeating myself, "I'M OFF".

As I began to walk out of the room, the doctor said that they will help me, and I need to see the crisis team at the mental health unit ASAP, I then left the room, with May close behind me. I stood outside the hospital and lit up a cigarette, then May told me that on the way out the doctor said to her, that I will receive a phone call first thing in the morning from the crisis team.

May phoned for a taxi to take us home. About 10am I received a phone call from the crisis team, the guy introduced himself as Andy, and asked me how I was feeling. He said his team were keen on meeting me in person and asked when would be a convenient time for me to pop down. I said that they had to radio through for another car to take May to the hospital.

After another long wait, I was seen by a different doctor from before. She asked if I had drunk any alcohol, to which I replied four small bottles of lager. I had a breath test which came back negative, so that proved I wasn't under the influence of alcohol. I could come down anytime, so we arranged a meeting for 1pm. When I arrived at the gate I had to buzz on the intercom, and state my name so I could gain entry to the car park.

I was ten minutes early so I sat in my car, turned my music up loud, and had a cigarette. I was buzzing again, and I felt 10ft tall. This was a strange (but good) feeling, it's like being high as a kite on fresh air. I walked to the main entrance and buzzed on a second intercom, where a security guard let me in. I gave my name to the person at the desk and said that I had an appointment with the crisis team, he said someone would come and meet me shortly, and asked me to take a seat.

I sat there watching all these patients shuffling around like zombies, totally out of it on their medication, and thought to myself, "What the fuck am I doing here". I must have waited five to ten minutes before I was met by a lady, who introduced herself as Karen. She said for me to follow her to a room where I would be met by the doctor. We walked down a long corridor, up some stairs, through four security coded doors (this place was like Fort Knox), before we came to a room, where Karen asked me to take a seat, and the doctor would be with me shortly.

A few minutes later the doctor along with Karen arrived, he introduced himself (but I cannot remember his name) and they sat down. He asked me how was I feeling, to which I replied that I felt high as a kite. He then said that it states on his records that I'm on anti-depressants, he then said I must stop taking them immediately, as they were making me more manic. He then asked me many questions about what I've been doing that wasn't my normal behaviour.

I was a bit reluctant to say about the online Lingerie, especially in front of Karen, but had to say that was one thing that wasn't my normal behaviour. He then asked me if I would be willing to try mood stabilisers, I said I was willing to try anything that might help. So he gave me two different types of meds, and said that I would need to have a blood test, and I hate blood tests. I asked if I could have the blood test done there, as I wanted to get it over and done with. So they called in a nurse, to do the test, but she couldn't do it, as I kept tensing up, so I had to have it done at a later date.

They said to me that they wanted to see me every other day, but wanted to speak to me on the phone every day. After a couple of days of taking these meds, they kicked in, and boy did they kick in. I was walking around the house like a zombie, I could not function at all. It was like I was somebody else, I looked at my reflection in the mirror and I saw a complete stranger looking back at me. I woke up one morning to take Mason to school, but I had to go straight back to bed again, so he missed school that day. I told the crisis team that I couldn't function properly on these meds, so they changed them to something different. After a week or so the new meds weren't quite as bad as the old ones, but I still didn't feel right.

One night I felt really bad, my head was racing, and I got quite worried. I decided to phone the crisis team emergency number that they gave me, to ask if I could come to the hospital. They said that would be fine and they will be expecting me. I called a taxi, as I didn't feel well enough to drive, and said to May that it would be best for her to stay at home. She said that she wanted to come, but I told her it was pointless as the hospital won't let her come in with me. So I convinced her to stay at home and went to pack some toiletries.

On arriving at the hospital, I spoke on the intercom and they said that they were expecting me, and opened the door. I was met by the security guard and a nurse who walked me to a locked door. Just as I was about to walk through the door my phone rang, and it was May. She said that she couldn't just sit at home and let me deal with this on my own, so she would be coming down to the hospital. I said this to the nurse, who then spoke to May on the phone, and told her to come tomorrow as she won't be allowed in tonight. I then spoke to May and told her I would see her tomorrow, then I had to ring off.

I went through the door where it shut quite loudly behind me, then was locked. I was then searched and they removed my tobacco and lighter, I asked them when I could have them back, and was quite abruptly told by a nurse that there was no smoking on this wing. If you have ever seen the film, 'One Flew Over The Cuckoo's Nest', there was a nurse in it called nurse Ratched, well, she reminded me of her.

Great, so now I couldn't even have a smoke. They led me to one room where I had to fill in a questionnaire before I was led to another room to be examined by a doctor. I was in there for ages, they were pricking my finger with a needle for a blood sample, taking my shoes and socks off, and checking my feet, checking my reflexes, there was no stone left unturned.

I finally got out of there around 3am where I was shown to my room. I was then woken up by two nurses with some tablets and a plastic cup of water. I asked what the tablets were, and they told me they were vitamins, but I wasn't convinced they were but took them anyway. I asked if there was somewhere I could go for a smoke, but was told again that was a non-smoking wing. The nurses said that I could ask for an inhaler or gum at the desk, and said I could have something to eat in the canteen.

I hate inhalers but I suppose it's better than nothing. I walked to the desk, where there were 2 people in front of me, I sat in a chair while I was waiting, and a woman came and sat next to me. I noticed the people in front were having more meds given to them, and thought perhaps they missed theirs earlier. Then the woman sat next to me said, "I like your jeans", to which I replied, "Thanks" while trying not to laugh. It was my turn at the desk, the woman handed me more meds with a cup of water, I said I'd already had them, but she said these were different that they were iron tablets, so I took them as well.

Then she asked me if I needed anything else, and I replied I would have half an ounce of Golden

Virginia and a pack of green rizla please. The woman that was sitting next to me nearly fell off her chair with laughter, but the one at the desk just gave me a bewildered look, so I said I was only joking, I would have an inhaler, some people have no sense of humour. I then headed for the canteen, where I had a couple of sandwiches. I was told by one of the nurses that the doctors would want to see me soon, and she would let me know when they were ready.

    I then went and sat in the lounge area, where they had the TV on. There were about four people in the room that were either asleep or talking. I asked them if they minded me putting some music on that I had on my phone. They said they didn't mind as no one was watching the TV, so I turned the music on and had the volume low.

A few minutes later nurse Ratched came in and said I wasn't allowed to have music on, when I said why, she said it might upset other people that were trying to watch the TV. I said that I had already asked everyone if they minded, and they said it was ok as they were not watching it, but she still said it wasn't allowed. So for the people that saw the film "One Flew Over The Cuckoo's Nest" will know what I mean about nurse Ratched.

An hour or two passed, then the nurse came in and said the doctors were ready to see me. She led me to a room where there were around eight people sitting at a long table, one of them was the psychiatrist I saw with the crisis team. They told me to take a seat, and asked how was I feeling, I said I was fine until nurse Ratched stole my tobacco and banned me from playing music, otherwise, I was ok. I heard some chuckles come from a couple of the doctors, then one of them asked the psychiatrist if I had been diagnosed, he then replied, "Yes it's bipolar disorder".

They said I could stay another night if I felt that I needed to, or if I felt well enough I could go home. I replied that I was well enough to go home, so the doctors said they would discharge me. At the exit they gave me my belongings, and I thanked nurse Ratched for her kind hospitality, in my own words. When I got outside I lit up a much-welcomed cigarette, phoned May, then got a taxi home.

When I arrived and spoke to May, she told me she was at the hospital for most of the night as well. I said to her, "What do you mean", and she replied that she came down there, despite knowing they would not let her in. She then said she sat in the waiting room for hours, and they still wouldn't let her see me, so she walked over to the main part of the hospital to buy a drink, and then she collapsed and got rushed into the hospital. She had picked up an infection and had to be put on a monitor. All this was going on and I didn't even know, I felt guilty and blamed myself for this. I was supposed to be caring for May, but I'm just adding more stress to what she already had, sometimes I think it might be better for everyone if I wasn't here.

I was seeing the crisis team on a regular basis for a month, and struggling with the meds, for the same amount of time. I was then transferred to the first response team, but shortly after that, I stopped taking the meds. I was doing fairly well at the time when May said to me that she had been thinking about buying a parrot. We had a bit of money, as May had a disability payment that had come through. The reason she had this idea is because many years ago I fell in love with some baby hand reared parrots that we saw in a pet shop. May also thought that this would be good therapy for me, to teach him certain tricks, she thought that it would keep my mind occupied.

So we had a long hard think about it and decided to buy a rainbow lorikeet, which is a fairly small parrot native to Australia. We decided to call him Jester, which was a perfect name for this species of parrot, as they are colourful clowns. Both May and I was very excited, and were eagerly awaiting his arrival. As soon as we got him, we all fell in love with the little fella, he was so sweet and loving from day one.

Mirror Mirror On The Wall
Please tell me who's looking back at me, before I fall.

Two pieces of the jigsaw puzzle that fit perfectly.
My dad aged 27, and I aged 23.
Quite spooky really.

Jester had settled in well, all seemed fine for a while, but I started to get bored again. Kayleigh showed me a face swap app that you could swap your face with almost anyone you wanted. So I had an idea, I'm going to take videos of me swapping faces with celebrity's, then post them on YouTube. I then setup a YouTube account and started to make a few videos, my kids (especially Mason) were embarrassed when they found out what I was doing, and asked me to delete them. I thought why should I delete them, I'm only having a bit of fun and it's not hurting anyone.

I started to film myself at any time of the day or night, one particular video I did at 4am, as I wanted to make them when no one else was around. Some people might find them funny, and some people won't, it depends on what sort of sense of humour you have. They are still on YouTube, so for all you people with the same sense of humour as me, that would like to view my short videos, Just type 'Clive Webb face swap' on YouTube but WARNING, the Peter Cook video contains highly offensive language throughout.

One evening I was having a smoke and started coughing, and thought about trying an e-cigarette, so the next morning I ordered an e-cig kit. First time using it I was very impressed, so much so I had an idea. I'm going to create a website to give my honest reviews on e-cigs, and the e-liquid that goes in them. So I set up my website, and wrote a review on the one I bought. Then I thought I can't just review one, I've got to be able to compare different types of e-cigs.

So I sent an email to the managing director of the company where I purchased mine. This is the email I sent to him, but I've cut out his name, and the name of the company, for obvious reasons.

Hi ****

I'm a fairly new customer of yours and as you know I've recently signed up as an affiliate. I was a smoker for nearly 35 years and thought it's about time to try and quit. It's been almost 2 weeks now where I haven't had a roll up using your e-cig. I have found the product brilliant, (apart from the odd leaky cart), in fact, I would not be lying in saying I find it better than the real thing. My wife is registered disabled with emphysema along with other illnesses, which I am her full-time carer. She has been a heavy smoker for nearly as long as me, which is the cause of her illnesses.

I thought it would be a good idea to write a review of my findings on a website in the hope it might help others. I'm new to all this but I've got a free website which I'm still working on. I've put a short review on there about the e-cig but still need to add more regarding this product. Now you probably get inundated with this sort of request, but

I was wondering if you would consider sending us other products for reviewing. I would love to add as many reviews as possible, but there is only the one as these are honest reviews. It's early days yet but my wife is trying the e-cig and at the moment has cut down on smoking by half. I will be adding all this to my website when I know what I'm doing a bit more. I look forward in hearing from you.

Kind regards,
Clive.

Dear Mr Webb.

At ***** request, I will send you our top of the range vaporiser and a sample pack of all our E-liquids. I see that you are ordering 1.8%...would that be okay?

Also please confirm that we should ship to the following address for you. If you get back to me before 15.00 I can ship today!

N/A ** ****** ***** ********

**** ***

Regards *****

I couldn't believe they sent me all of this free of charge, this would have cost nearly £200. I sent them an email back to thank them and say that I would review all that they had sent as soon as possible. After I did the reviews, I was going to email different companies to ask them the same, but then I got bored with the idea, and deleted my website.

Going back to my little friend Jester, he used to love snuggling into my hand or neck, especially after he had a bath. He used to roll over on his back to play fight with me, but he would be very gentle. Then I noticed he started to change towards me, he started to lunge at me and bite, this would be out of the blue, and for no apparent reason. I was not feeling myself, and he knew this.

One particular day he was sitting on my arm chatting away, as a happy content bird does, then he flew at my face biting me in the eye. I jumped up out of my seat in pain, he must have got a fright and flew on top of his cage, squawking loudly. I rushed out of the room and headed for the kitchen clutching my eye, I did not want to take my hand away, as I was convinced that there would have been blood, and I would need hospital treatment for an eye injury. But I was panicking for nothing, all I had was a scratch on my eyelid, and blurred vision for a couple of days.

After that, I was very wary of Jester when he got anywhere near my face, and I think he picked up on this. I couldn't make it out, why is he was acting like this when he had been so gentle and loving before. Don't get me wrong, he had his good days, but he could just change when I was least expecting it. This started to really affect me, I wasn't in a good place, and I was thinking 'should I relocate him?' This would devastate me if I had to give him up, and I would burst into tears at the thought of it.

One minute I would go to his cage to speak to him, and give him a head scratch, and he would be fine, the next he would back away from me, and give me a look like he wanted to attack. He was looking at me like he did not recognise me, I was a complete stranger to him. This was actually a bit of a coincidence, as I didn't recognise me either. I would look in the mirror, and wonder who the fuck is that staring back at me.

They say that birds can sense our moods, and the way we feel, and I think they are right, but like I said with Jester when he looks at me in the eyes, it's like he is seeing someone else. I still don't know what is going to be the outcome with Jester, I just hope that we can rekindle the bond that we once had, before he could see the green eyed monster that was within me.

I now have been back to see my doctor and we have agreed that I would go back and see the first response team. One road I do not want to go down is the medication that slaughtered me.

Summary

Well I'm up to date with my life now, it's quite a short book when I think this is my life story. I've probably missed some parts of my life, which I've either forgotten or wiped out of my mind. My mum always said to me I'm so much like my dad, in looks and in my ways. I never thought I looked like him, until I put the two photos together, that was quite spooky.

Now I've pieced this jigsaw puzzle together (which is my life), I'm still missing quite a few pieces, but I can see what the picture is. I can see my dad as a little boy lost, but no one could understand him, not even his own parents. All the ideas he had, like start his own business, then either couldn't cope or got bored with it (just like me). Start a project and spend days, if not weeks on, then get bored and discard it (just like me), start a new job that he normally wouldn't take, then only last a few months because he got bored with it (just like me).

I was told, "Oh that's just the way your dad was", NO, these were manic episodes that went undetected. Me with the jet-skis, the shop, the websites etc, were manic episodes. You can see where I'm going with this, my dad didn't decide to become a human torch just out of depression alone. He had other mental issues like I've been diagnosed with having, don't get me wrong, I have no thoughts of taking my own life.

As Luke Skywalker said in Star Wars, "The force (mental illness in my case) is strong in my family, my father had it, I have it, and my sister has it", yes sis you have it too. Sometimes I think to myself, "If only I was a lot older on that fateful day with my dad, I might have been able to save him". He tried to take his own life on two previous occasions, if that is not a cry for help, then I don't know what is. It's quite scary when I think that I'm 51, the same age as my dad when it happened.

What I have found out is that mania is like a wild horse. I've named this mad white stallion "White Lightning", and I'm trying to tame and break him in. I've managed to get a saddle and reins on him, so now I will be able to ride White Lightning, and control the pace and direction he is going. But he is a feisty beast, and doesn't like to be controlled. But I'm hoping (giving time) that we both can learn to respect one another, and he doesn't give me too much of a bumpy ride.

I'm sure on some occasions, I'm going to lose grip of the reins and fall off, and hopefully, I will be able to get up and dust myself off, with the help of my family. The green eyed monster is the depression, he has no name as I don't want to be familiar with him. I'm still not sure how to tame this beast, as he is very unpredictable, and shows up unannounced at any time, night, or day. As you might have guessed, I've been riding White Lightning whilst writing this book. I was nearly at the finish line, when the monster showed up and ripped the reins from my hands.

Who knows what lies around the corner, if we knew this, at least we could duck from the boot that was just about to kick us in the head. I'd like to take this opportunity to thank you all for reading my book, and I hope you enjoyed it. I'm very surprised and pleased with myself for finishing this story, as normally I would have gotten bored after just a few pages.

Everything in this book is true and from my heart, nothing has been added that hasn't happened to me. I would appreciate any questions, comments, or a review on Amazon. You never know, I might write another book if I can come to a mutual agreement with White Lightning, and Mr Green Eyes.

Little Boy Lost poem

The little boy is crying, he is lost and all alone. The little boy is crying, he saw his dad burn his home. The little boy is crying, he cried himself to sleep. The little boy is crying, as he lay on the wet sheet. The little boy is crying, he was dragged by his hand. The little boy is crying, crying inside the man. The little boy is crying, he is hurt and in pain. The little boy is crying, he's riding White Lightning again. The little boy is crying, when he looks in the mirror to see. The little boy is crying, is that reflection you dad? Or is it me.

That's all for now folks,

Best wishes,

Clive.

I'd like to thank all my family, May, Grant, Kayleigh, and Mason, for their support over the past couple of years. I know I've been a pain in the butt, :-) love you all.

Printed in Great Britain
by Amazon